I0567307

Investing for Beginners

Transform Your Life and Get Rich Before Retirement

(Learn Stock Market, Forex, Options Trading and Futures)

Nancy Green

Published By **Jordan Levy**

Nancy Green

Investing for Beginners: Transform Your Life and Get Rich Before Retirement (Learn Stock Market, Forex, Options Trading and Futures))

ISBN 978-1-998769-40-7

Legal & Disclaimer

The information contained in this ebook is not designed to replace or take the place of any form of medicine or professional medical advice. The information in this ebook has been provided for educational & entertainment purposes only.

The information contained in this book has been compiled from sources deemed reliable, and it is accurate to the best of the Author's knowledge; however, the Author cannot guarantee its accuracy and validity and cannot be held liable for any errors or omissions. Changes are periodically made to this book. You must consult your doctor or get professional medical advice before using any of the suggested remedies, techniques, or information in this book.

Table Of Contents

Introduction 1

Chapter 1: Invest Or Save, Which Is Better? 6

Chapter 2: How To Invest With Index Funds 12

Chapter 3: What Are Futures Trading?... 27

Chapter 4: Stockmarket 44

Chapter 5: Guide To Swing Trading 62

Chapter 6: Start Soon, But Start Small.... 81

Chapter 7: What Is Network Marketing And How Does It Work? 88

Chapter 8: Portfolio Building................ 100

Chapter 9: Social Investing, What Is It? 107

Chapter 10: The Process Of Moving In . 127

Chapter 11: Set Your Personal Finance Principles 144

Chapter 12: Expert Trading Options 151

Chapter 13: Alternative Trading Options
.... 155

Chapter 14: Active Income Vs Passive
Income... 161

Chapter 15: Habits Of Investing: Getting
Used To It... 166

Introduction

When we think of investment, we often picture large amounts of money being traded on banks, securities and stocks. Some people are afraid of investing. Many people think that investment is reserved for those who are wealthy and want to make more. This is because investment is a term that often refers to actual money. However, investments go beyond money. It can be an asset you own that you use to exchange for something else to gain more.

The idea of investment was born long ago. History shows that investment was a concept that existed in ancient times without people knowing it would have a profound impact on the future. The Christian Bible has the concept investment in ancient scriptures. Jesus spoke of three servants receiving bags of gold. In the parable, two servants used the golds to gain more. But the other man decided that he would dig a hole and hide his money. The Code of Hammurabi also shows early people's understanding of the importance of investment. This was a law from 1700 BCE that required land to be pledged as collateral for investment. These examples demonstrate how important investing in the current society is. Investing is the only way for them to make more of what little they do have.

The practice continued up to 1602. Amsterdam saw the opening of the first global stock exchange. This changed the investment landscape. Amsterdam Stock Exchange was a platform that connected potential investors to businesses and projects that would allow them to make more of their investment. This is when terms such liquidity, low transaction costs and publicized value were introduced to the financial industry. Because of the creation and operation of stock exchanges throughout Europe, investments became more accessible and standardised.

During the Industrial Revolution people realized they needed to save their earnings. This mindset led to the rise of the European banking industry. The banking industry allowed people to save money and place it in savings for the future. JP Morgan, Lehman Brothers, as well as other financial institutions, were built over the years. These institutions were able to sell millions of dollars worth bonds and help the federal government finance weapons, machinery, and other equipment for the American Civil War. International investments were possible, thus the concept of international investing was born. Financial institutions understand that they have greater potential to do what they can within their country. They believe they can achieve greater success in the global market.

The success of financial institutions worldwide is not due to the amount of money they have. In reality, money is only a tool that investors can use. These institutions have been strengthened to the point that they can manipulate the entire economy of a country. The businessmen and investors who make financial institutions possible won't allow them to succeed in the marketplace. They play a critical role in the success and failure of investments.

The question is, however, still open for these financial experts. Are there any business strategies or habits they had that allowed them to succeed in the finance and banking industry? As we all know, their assets are the most powerful tool they have. Most people assume that investments are only made of money. Money is a key tool in investments. However, money can also be assets like land or property that can be used for collateral.

Businessmen and investors have their core strategy and their habits. Your attitude towards assets is the key to unlocking your potential. Are you an aggressive investor or a conservative one. This book shares the common knowledge and jargon that investors use when entering the financial market. This book will show you that investment does not have to be about how much money you have. It can take many forms. This book will teach you how to plan and execute strategies to make sure your money goes where it belongs. This book will help you to see the common 7 habits that successful investors use in order to gain a better perspective on investment strategies. So, what are you waiting? Let's invest in our future and get started!

Chapter 1: Invest Or Save, Which Is Better?

Do you often wonder whether it is better to save money or invest? Your goals and financial situation are key factors in determining the right answer. We'll be looking at how to save money, increase savings, invest wisely, and what you can do to make your money work hard for you.

What is the difference of savings and investment?

Investing simply means trading the money you have today in exchange for more money in future. It is placing your money in investments to help it grow and provide a good return. However, you can also invest your money in a home or business purchase.

Simple definition: Saving is "isolating" money that you keep aside to prevent spending. You can put your savings aside in a banking account.

What are you supposed to save for?

It is essential to learn how to save money before investing. Before you begin investing your money, here are two things to consider:

1.

You need to be prepared in case of an emergency.

It is crucial to keep an emergency fund aside and be prepared for all eventualities. At least three months worth of your monthly living expenses should be saved. This will give you financial security. This is the foundation of your financial security.

2.

Continue Savings to keep your energy high

After you've established an emergency savings fund, it is time to start saving money each month.

Your expenses will determine the answer, but it is a good rule of thumb to save 10% of your monthly earnings.

After some time, and once you have enough savings, you will be able to start thinking about how you can invest. The type and amount of investment you want will impact the time it takes for you to save. To invest in real estate, for example, you will need to save a bit more. However, if your goal is to make a start now with as little money as $100, you will need to save more.

Are you ready to make an investment?

The key to investing terms is determining your investment goals and horizon. The term of an investment will have a significant impact on your tolerance for risk. It is also determined by how the money will be used and when. To avoid volatile investments, it is better to place your money in a savings or certificate of deposit account, rather than in the stock market.

Let's look at some common terms in the next few lines.

1. Short-term goals

These are the five goals you wish to achieve in the next 5 years. You have plenty of options to short-term invest that provide decent returns and help you reach your short term goals. These investments are safer than long term investments such as stocks if your investor style is conservative. They typically yield returns in less that 5 years or sometimes within a year. These are some short-term options for investors looking to maximize profits, minimize risk and reduce risks.

* Certificate Of Deposit

* Treasury Securities

* Bond Funds

* Peer-to-Peer Lending

* Money Market account

* Online Savings Card

Because of its volatility and high cost, we don't recommend you invest in the stock markets as your short goals. Investing in stock markets should be part or your long-term goal

(10 years or longer), assuming that you have sufficient savings and other income sources to finance your expenses.

"Beware: Stock market fluctuations are common. If you do not plan to invest for more than five years, you could lose significant capital."

2. Medium-term goals

These are the long-term goals you wish to achieve in the next 5-10 years. These goals are the link between your short-term and long-term objectives.

Investments for medium-term goals tend to be less conservative than long investments, but are more risk-tolerant that short-term options. Medium-term investment seeks to find a balance of return and risk.

3. Long-term objectives

These are long-term plans that you won't be required to withdraw money in the next ten years.

Long-term financial goals are more realistic when it comes to investing. This is because inflation can significantly impact the value of your cash savings.

The stock market has a tendency to be more successful over the long-term, which gives you the opportunity to earn higher returns on your investment. People with large amounts of extra cash can invest more in the stock market, as we have already mentioned.

Chapter 2: How To Invest With Index Funds

You have now learned the basics of investing. Let's take a look at how to make your first investments. You don't have to worry if there are any questions you still have, or if you're unsure about where to start. These are the types of questions that this chapter and the next chapter can help you answer.

Here are five steps to take note of before you begin

In a nutshell: There are five main steps you should remember when investing in index fund funds.

1. Learn as many details as you possibly can about index funds. I have already mentioned the importance research and learning as much as you possibly can about investing. This applies also to index funds. You have already learned a few things about index funds in this book. However, there are still many more. You should continue to do your

research and find out as much information as you can. The book's end will give you additional reading material to help you continue your journey.

2. Compare the fees charged and the companies. You can compare what you learn as you go along with your research. Take a list with the companies you are most interested in and make a comparison. Keep in mind the inflation rate and compare the fees offered by companies.

3. Consider the benefits ETFs may bring to your investment. I already talked about the similarities and differences between ETFs (index funds) and ETFs (ETFs). These two are often inseparable and many people will look to ETFs or index funds as a way to save money. As an index investor, it's always beneficial to take into consideration how ETFs may benefit you.

4. Make sure you are ready to open a trading account before you do. This is one step that you don't have to be ready for. A lot of

experienced investors will tell beginners that they should only open accounts when they are fully ready to start investing.

5. You can buy regularly and reinvest your dividends. Don't be alarmed if you don't purchase anything for a few weeks. You don't need to buy multiple investments at once. Instead, make sure you are buying index funds every day. Also, reinvest any dividends received from funds you own into your fund. This will help you increase your investments which will lead to more savings over time.

Deciding Where to Purchase

There are many factors to consider when buying an index fund. A mutual fund company, or a trust broker can help you purchase an index funds. You will need to pay attention not only to trading costs but also convenience and fund selection.

In addition to trading costs, it is also worth looking into any fees that a broker/company will charge you when you invest with them. A commission-free option is another thing you should look at. ETFs are sometimes offered without commission by brokers. You may find it helpful to find a trusted broker with no commission if your first investment is not financially feasible.

Convenience is what you want. You want someone you can trust, who can explain the investing process and someone who can be your one-stop source. People of all ages are busy, so they don't have to spend much time going from one place in order to invest. You'll also want to find someone who you can stick with for as long time as possible.

Sometimes, a broker can provide a list of funds that are available for you to choose from. Before you decide to work with a broker to invest in different companies, you should investigate the possibility.

Reviewing the costs

Before buying an index fund you should be aware of the costs.

Your fund will subtract the expense from your return to calculate your expense ratio. This fee is what the market charges for their participation in the process. This is a cost that you can't ignore. However these fees are often lower in index funds than for active-type funds. The index fund expense rate average cost is 0.8%. However, an average expense ratio of an active fund is over 0.50%.

An investment minimum can be defined as the minimum amount that you can contribute to an index fund for it to be bought. Prices will vary depending on the type and price of the fund. While some funds can be as low as a few hundred dollars, others may cost you closer to $2,000.

The tax cost factor is an expense which is added to the expense ratio or other fees. This is due to an increase in your annual income. The expense must be reported on your taxes to the International Revenue Service. You cannot ignore this expense or try to get it waived. In most cases, you only have to pay 0.3% to 0.5% off your return amount.

A minimum account fee is a fee you may be charged by a broker, or any other person for opening a new market account. This fee is separate from the investment minimal and can sometimes not be considered. It all depends on what fees the broker charges.

Keep an eye out for your Portfolio

I've already discussed the importance of your portfolio in the previous chapter. However, I want to remind you that while your portfolio is important, it should not be neglected. Your portfolio holds all of your investments. In a way, your portfolio is your resume. It will help you to show others that you are serious about investing if you ever decide to make it a career.

How can you ensure your portfolio is well-managed? The type of investor you're depends partly on this. You'll spend more time looking after your portfolio if it's a serious investor. But if you invest to earn extra money for retirement, you might not pay as much attention to your portfolio.

Your portfolio type will also influence how often you need to check it. You will need to check your portfolio daily if you are investing in individual stocks. The stock market will also be closely monitored by you if you are interested in reading news from other sources. But if you invest in an Index, you don't have the obligation to pay weekly or monthly attention to your portfolio. Your schedule is up to you, but it is important that your portfolio be inspected at least once a calendar year.

When is the best time of year to buy?

Part of the answer to this question depends on how serious you are about investing. For those who plan to invest for the long-term, it is best to buy during the year. There are criteria that can be used to help people who invest in index funds to determine the best time for them to buy funds.

You should not buy index fund bonds when the economy is weakest. If you are interested in purchasing stocks, it is best to do so when the stock price is rising. This does not mean that people are buying the stock, but that the company is in a good place.

Steps to Take When Investing In Index Funds

1. You'll need to submit your banking information

You will need your banking information to open your investment account. This information is critical. It is essential that you have a good relationship with the person to whom you are providing your information. To put it another way, make sure you only share your information with your trusted broker and only give him or her what he/she needs. You must provide this information because returns to your bank account will be sent.

2. Check that you meet the Minimum Requirements

Many index funds require minimum investments of at least $3,000. The average minimum investment is $3,000. However, the index fund fee must be paid before you can start saving money.

It doesn't take long to find the best index fund for you. It may take you longer to find the right index fund. The market will provide the minimum requirements for an index fund. You can search this market to find them. Keep in mind that not all minimum requirements fees are equal. However, they typically range from approximately $2,000 to about $3,000.

3. All Fees Must Be Paid

Each index fund will have its own fees. Each fund has its own fees. They will vary in expense ratios, with the best ones being 0.1% or 0.2%. If you don't pay attention and take note of the fees, you could be caught off guard when you get a return.

This is in addition to making sure you pay all fees up front. It's convenient because once fees have been paid, you don't have to worry about how much money you will need to continue paying them. Instead, you can let your investments grow while you relax.

4. An ETF could be the best place to start

Some people find it hard to pay the minimum fee for index investing. Others don't have the money they need to purchase an index. Investors advise that you consider buying an ETF first if you find yourself in this position. You can wait until your first purchase, or you can focus on saving money. However, investing in an ETF is a great way start your investing journey.

An ETF allows for you to buy an index from a reliable company, such S&P 500 or Microsoft. These companies are considered the best to invest in as they have been stable for a long duration. Additionally, they are considered blue-chip businesses and charge a low annual fee. You still need to ensure you can afford to invest.

5. Take a look to the Returns

A key aspect of investing is the return you will receive from an index funds. You will get the highest returns on index funds that have a small capitalization. Keep in mind that just because the company is larger does not guarantee you will receive the highest return. Experiential investors will tell ya that the smaller-capitalized companies are more likely to see the greatest returns, as the company is growing. Today, the best small capitalized companies to see the greatest returns are iShares Russell 2000ETF (IWM), Vanguard Russell 2000ETF (VTWO), S&P600 Small Cap ETFs (SLY).

6. Find a company that offers several index funds

Not only do you need to ensure your company can afford an index fund but also that they have enough funds. You should also ensure you choose the best index fund for your needs. You might choose a mutual fund if you are certain that you will make smaller investment into the index funds after you have met your minimum requirement. BlackRock and Vanguard are among the top index funds companies that offer many options.

7. Compare the Fees that you pay with the expected Returns

Once you start investing you'll be able find the quote for the expected returns based on what was paid to buy the index fund. But you'll need to find out the expected return, and how it differs from the purchase cost of the index funds. For financial stability, it is important to compare the price of the index fund to determine if the expected return will be equal. It is the return that exceeds the fees that makes index funds the best to invest in.

8. You can make one-time investment through a broker

It is important to know what fees the broker charges if you choose to go this route. You may be charged a flat fee if you add money to an index fund. Consider other options if your plans include adding money to the index fund often. A broker is your best option if you intend to invest a lump amount or add to an Index annually.

9. Diversifying your Portfolio: Find the Right Balance

This book will explain how index funds can benefit and hinder your portfolio diversification. This is one area in which investors don't agree. Some investors believe that diversifying could harm your portfolio. Others believe that diversifying may be beneficial to your portfolio. The type of portfolio you are creating will play a part in this. To have a balanced portfolio, you need to choose the right balance. It can increase your income over the course of time. However, diversifying your portfolio can also make it more difficult. This is something you should discuss with your broker or advisor.

10. You must monitor the progress and performance of your investment

As I have discussed, monitoring your investment progress can either be helpful or detrimental. This depends on how often your monitors are updated. But it is vital that you watch your investments. The progress of index funds is generally stable, so it's not necessary to keep an eye on it every week. Many investors agree that you don't need check on progress monthly. You can check the progress of your Index Fund every six months to annually due to its stability.

It is worth taking the time to keep an eye on your index fund and comparing it with other funds. It is possible to switch your fund if an index fund of a different fund performs better than you. But you shouldn't do it immediately. Compare different funds over time and take note of the expected returns. It is vital that you do not jump to switch index funds or worry if another index fund is performing better. This is a sign that you are losing control and your emotions. It is important to maintain control of your emotions.

If you are concerned that your index fund isn't performing as well, consider trading it or simply cashing out. A broker will usually charge additional fees for switching to or cashing out. You should be aware of these fees.

11. Continue to add to your Index Fund

You don't necessarily have to make additional money after your initial deposit. But many investors advise you to do so. It will not only increase the principal but also increase your returns. You can always add to your index funds as much or as little as you like. When your annual check is done on your index, you can decide to save more or to invest more. You can also invest money quarterly or once a month. There is no one right answer as to how often money should be added to your investments. However, fees will need to be considered when adding money to your investment.

Chapter 3: What Are Futures Trading?

People are often confused about futures trading. Most people assume that futures trading involves extreme financial risk. While these things may seem to go hand in hand with futures trading, it is not true. What is the purpose of trading futures? Futures are contracts for a specific commodity to be delivered at a future date. Some commodities that are commonly traded include agricultural commodities like wheat, soybeans and rice. Metals such as copper, zinc, yellow, and currencies are also included.

Futures trading is a completely different type of investing than many other types. This is because futures traders are not required to purchase or own the commodity. Trader's trading decision is made by speculating the price of a commodity. If the trader believes the price will rise, then he will purchase the commodity. Similar to the previous example, he might sell futures contracts if the price falls. If his prediction proves true, he'll make money from the trade. His prediction will be correct, but he may lose.

Speculators trade large amounts of future contracts. Most of them either make profits or suffer losses before the contract expires. The investor is not responsible for delivering the commodity during such transactions. Speculators play an important role in the economy as they trade large volumes of commodities which has an effect on the price movements. In order to have a clear picture about price movements, it's important to monitor trading volumes. Additionally, speculators make planning for the future easier for those who take delivery of the commodity. The true buyers and sellers are reassured that there are always other people in the market who can buy or sell the contract.

Trading futures requires a lot of learning. A reputable futures broker with a strong track record is recommended if you want to trade futures. Choose the commodity which you wish to trade. You should also keep an eye out for price movements in the market to determine your trading position. For a trading position that is consistent with these indicators, you should use historical price charts, patterns, and other important indicators such as moving average prices and moving mean convergence divergence (MACD).

To determine the trading hours, contract month and last trading day, make sure you always read the contract specifications. Trade futures can give you valuable experience. There are always high losses for beginners. Trade with a practice trading account to gain enough experience and knowledge before moving into real trading. Practice accounts are updated in real time and provide data and price movements. You can therefore gain valuable knowledge and experience while not losing any money.

You can start by making a small investment to get familiar with futures trading. This will minimize your risk. Be disciplined in your trading and don't panic if there are losses. Analyze your strategy to make changes if necessary. After a while, you will start to make decent income and will no longer wonder what futures trading is. It's not difficult to become a pro at futures trading.

Futures Trading in Currencies vs. Futures Trading in Stock Market

A broker or agent is required to handle all transactions in the stock market, as well as receiving price quotes. Forex futures trading is free from the need for an agent or middleman, and therefore these costs are non-existent. This reduces the risk of losing money and increases investor margins. For high volume traders, these brokerage fees can add up to significant amounts.

Portfolios are a good way to keep track of past investments and track profits from various trades. This tracker allows investors speculate on future investments.

Both futures are generally the same. Forex futures are traded on multiple exchanges worldwide. However, most Forex futures can be traded via the Chicago Mercantile Exchange as well as its partnering brokers.

Forex charts allow investors to view past market trends. They also help in forecasting future outcomes. Trend forecasting isn't always accurate. Returns are not always guaranteed, but this is a common problem for any type trading. Investors need to monitor the charts for "predicting oscillators", which will help them anticipate swings.

Even though there is no commission or transaction fee, investors and traders will still be affected by the spread. Spread refers to the difference between buying and selling currencies. This can be used in Forex futures trading as well as regular Forex Trading. Research has shown that Forex futures trading is still the most lucrative form.

Both futures trade in currencies or stocks have both their benefits and drawbacks.

Research and assessments have shown that futures trading in currencies is less volatile than stock exchange trading. This decreases the possibility of high profits or high loss. Forex futures trading is a good option for risk-averse traders. It's also more profitable than the stock market over the long-term. Many people also use it as a hedge to currency fluctuations.

Futures trading and commodity trading were first established in Japan and Holland around 18th century. Commodity trading in the USA began with the establishment of a commodity market in the 1840s. This market offered both futures contracts and sport delivery.

Futures trading differs in some aspects from spot trading. Spot trades are for real-time cash/product deliveries, futures are traded to hedge possible price uncertainties. Spot trading is usually done with a 2-day cash delivery method. Futures trades last for 3 months. Spot trades are contracts that expire in the next month or less.

Meat, grains, and live stocks were among the first products to be offered for futures trading. The introduction of futures contracts for a variety more products was possible later, including for metals, currencies, stocks, stock indexes, private and government rates, as well as for energy products, commodities, metals, currencies, currency indexes, stocks, and other products. CME (Chicago Mercantile Exchange), is responsible for the introduction and rapid growth of financial features.

Futures are guaranteed by clearinghouses and have fixed contract specifications. These specifications are also margined to limit counterparty credit risk. They can be traded through an open outcry or screen in public domain. Futures contracts have a lot in common with forward contracts. The names of the contracts are often used interchangeably. However, forwards contracts are generally traded OTC (over the counter) through broker/dealer interactions or issuer-client relationships, while futures are traded through centralized marketplaces.

Commodity futures are one of the most commonly traded futures. Futures trading is now possible for new commodities, such as agricultural and livestock products. Futures options offer the ability to trade futures contracts at a given price at a particular time. They are similar to stock options. A call option allows you to purchase futures contracts, and a put option allows you to sell them.

Stock features (or single-stock) are futures contracts for the ownership of an underlying stock. Stock features typically have higher leverage and holders of futures don't receive any dividends. Stock index futures may be used for hedging or trading as well as investing. For those who want to own stocks or index options, hedgers, traders, and investors, but not for the direct ownership of the stock, they can be used for various purposes. Futures contracts with currency options allow holders to sell or buy a currency at a certain rate at a future date. Futures contracts are constantly marked-to market so that forex investors can easily avoid the obligation of selling or buying currencies before delivery.

The CFTC (Commodity Futures Trading Commission), governs futures trading. CBOT is Chicago Board of Trade; CME, ICE Futures; Euronext.liffe; London Commodity Exchange; Intrade, London Metal Exchange; TOCOM (Tokyo Commodity Exchange); NYMEX (New York Mercantile Exchange); NYBOT [New York Board of Trade], Sydney Futures Exchange); etc.

Futures Trading Brokers

If done properly, futures trading could prove to be a profitable venture. Before entering into futures trading it is crucial to contact the right broker, who will consider the best interests of trader. Research shows that nearly half of all the companies are currently in operation. They offer a range of services, from full service to discount service to online services. It is up to traders to decide which futures company they want, depending on how comfortable they are with stock markets.

Even though the trader may be familiar with stock market basics, futures trading is an entirely different arena and may require some professional advice. A full-service broker should be at least six year old. This broker can be a great help in establishing a profitable futures trading business. He can provide updates to his client on economic trends and efficient methods of trading. These brokers are more expensive than the rest, but they can make a significant profit for their clients. Trading can be made easy by the broker's experience and knowledge.

Traders may choose discounted futures trading businesses. While it may be cheaper, the broker will still provide the same services as full-time traders. It is best to continue trading with your old broker until the reliability and viability of the discount trading firm are analyzed.

Veteran traders are choosing to trade with online brokers for futures trading. They require continuous, reliable connectivity to perform different types of trading. Online firms receive lower commission rates. Online firms are not guaranteed profitability. However, it is essential that a professional monitors trade and recommends the best moves.

Cost is not the only thing that matters when choosing a futures trading firm. Futures trading is a delicate business. Experienced traders can avoid making unwise investments that could cause financial instability. This is not possible, but experienced brokers can reduce the risk and warn traders about potential pitfalls.

Futures Trading: Benefits

If we take a close look at the current business landscape, then it is easy to see that futures are growing in popularity. In fact, futures trading is the most commonly traded commodity on any market. The latest definitions of futures trading are that it is a trading of futures contracts. These contracts allow the owner to trade the basic commodity at some point in the future at a fixed rate. Futures trades can be made in the same way as options and stocks, but they are executed on centralized futures commodity markets. It can be divided into two types depending on the type, financial and commodity futures.

The physical delivery is what ends commodity futures contract trading. They could include agricultural commodity futures such as rice, oats or wheat. or energy commodity futures like natural gas, crude oil, etc. metals & stone like gold and silver, as well as diamonds. This means that when a futures trader's contract expires, the buyer will make the appropriate payments and the seller will deliver basic commodities (agricultural and energy). The trading of financial futures contract contracts is done with a cash settlement. It includes futures on treasury note, bonds, mutual fund, etc.

Electronic trading platforms can be used to trade futures contracts. Or, you can use the traditional open outcry method that is available on the floor of an exchange. It is important that the futures contract clearly states the physical delivery date and the location of the commodity. Exchanges may specify delivery arrangements from time to time. This is especially important when commodities have high transportation costs. This can affect the delivery area.

All commodity future traders must be aware of the daily price movement limits that are set by most exchanges for commodity futures contracts. A limit movement simply refers to any price move that moves in any direction other than the daily price limit. Limit down refers to a contract that is subject to price movements below the daily price limit. The contract is also considered limit down if the price moves below the limit. Prices limits and positions limits are designed to stop large price movements that can be caused by excessive speculation. These artificial barriers can be used to prevent traders from trading if the price is rapidly changing.

While trading in commodity futures is certainly a way to make good money, there are some important factors to consider. It is extremely volatile in nature and more susceptible to being unpredictable due to many factors like geopolitical worries, contracted demand–supply fundamentals growth and inflation that place pressure on the global commodities market. It is an interesting market environment, but also very dangerous. This market has seen many wars and many companies competing for food and natural resources.

Similarities between futures and options trading

What are the differences between options and futures trading? What are some commonalities? There are actually four main areas where options are similar to futures.

First, options as well as futures are both derivative instruments. These options and futures can be traded at specific prices to determine their value. Futures and options both only bind the exchange at a specified price. Options and futures wouldn't exist without an underlying assets. They are therefore known as derivative instruments. Futures and options are both created to facilitate the trading their underlying asset.

Second, both options as well as futures are leverage tools. Option trading and futures both allow you to control the price movement of their underlying assets better than your cash would. For example, a futures contract requiring a 10% margin would give you the ability to control tenx more of the asset's underlying assets than what your cash would normally permit. An option that asks for $1.00 to purchase a stock at $20 would give you twenty times the leverage. It allows you control a stock of $20 worth with $1. With leverage, you can make more profit on options and futures by buying the underlying asset using the same amount of money. Both sides of leverage are possible. Options and futures trading could result in you losing more than if your underlying asset were purchased.

Hedging can be done using both options or futures. One of the most important uses for derivatives is hedging. You can use options or futures to hedge the directional price risks of assets. Options, however, are more flexible and precise. Optional hedging allows you to profit even if the underlying asset experiences a strong breakout. The hedging power offered by options and futures is vital in helping to reduce the market's downward pressure during market crisis. Large institutions and funds have the option and/or potential to hedge the downside risks of their holdings with options and/or forwards rather than selling their shares. Downside pressure in the market can partly be relieved by reducing how much these big funds are selling. This doesn't stop bear markets forming when the general market crowd (aka "Herd") rushes out of the marketplace.

Fourth, both options as well as futures can be used for profit other than the price movement in the underlying stock. Futures spreads may be used to speculate on seasonal differences in the prices of futures contracts that have different expiration month. Options spreads can be designed to profit from the time decay of any underlying asset. Options strategies and futures strategy are what make derivatives trading so enjoyable and rewarding for those with the mathematical skills and strategies.

Options and futures can be very different derivative instruments. They also have different rules and trading characteristics. You can still be a smarter trader or investor if both options as well as futures.

Chapter 4: Stockmarket

Individuals who are relatively new to financial exchange speculators will have minimal learning and participation in the contributor circle. For the most part, these people follow a purchase and hold' exchanging approach. You are a tenderfoot if you have been involved in financial exchanges. You can only make a limited number of transactions per month with a money account. This doesn't necessarily mean that your requirements for financial exchange exchanging aren't high. Your curiosity and interest in expanding your knowledge as well as speculation involvement are likely to be a key part of achieving any goals you might have. It is all enjoyable and great.

It is not possible for youngsters to view timberland just from the trees. It is also difficult for them to determine if the future potential of a particular security is favorable, regardless whether exchanging patterns in the present are predictable. Apprentices are frequently competent during strong 'buyer' markets. It is surprising that many get confused in difficult events, particularly when market volatility is greater and the show is run by bears. If this is an event that you strongly believe you can fit, these are some financial exchange business nuts and bolts for students, which might be useful.

These are the most common mistakes

#1. Understanding the investment is not important

Warren Buffett (one of the best financial advisors in the world), warns against investing resources into organizations that don't receive it. This means that you should avoid buying stock in organizations if the plans of action are not clear to you.

#2 Falling in LOVE with a Particular Company

Every time we see an organization where we have invested resources well, it's difficult not to feel passionate emotions for it. We forget that we bought stock as a venture.

#3 Lack of Patience

How many times has gradual improvement proved to be an unavoidable fact? Gradual beats competition more often than not - whether you're at the gym or in school. It is not unreasonable to assume that it should be unique in how they contribute. A consistent, measured, and taught approach would go a lot further than just trying to be the best.

#4 Too many investment turnovers

Turnover, also known as hopping around in positions, is another arrival executioner. Unless your institution is a financial specialist with low commissions rates, exchange costs can ruin you. This includes the momentary assessment and open door costs of not taking up long-term gains of wise speculations.

It is essential to fully grasp that individuals must have different levels of hazard resilience. This is a clear indication that there is no "right equalization" in this matter.

It is common to notice a decrease of nervousness when you put resources or exchange securities. This is because of your 'view' on the potential dangers. This will give you the ability to abstain if you do not fully comprehend the hazard-resistance of the ventures. In a perfect universe, you should not invest your resources in an advantage. This can lead to restless nights. Tension triggers anxiety, which in turn leads to passionate reactions to stressors. You will be able to maintain calmness during securities exchange vulnerability and to adhere to an 'apathetically required leadership process in financial exchange exercises.

You should not allow your emotions to distract you from your ventures.

Amateurs must confront a significant obstacle: their inability or unwillingness to control their emotions and to make rational decisions. For now, the cost of stocks of organizations is correlated with the collective feelings of the entire venture network. The stock cost of an organization's stock will rise if the majority of securities exchange financial specialists are concerned about a certain firm. If most dealers hold a positive view of a company, then its stock cost will typically rise.

People with a pessimistic outlook on the securities exchange are known by the term 'bears. Those who are optimistic about the securities exchange are called "bulls." The constant battle between bears, bulls, and others during market hours focuses on the ever-changing protections' cost. These transient changes often result from gossip, hypotheses, or expectation. These elements can be described as emotions. A legitimate and efficient investigation of the company's potential benefits, the board and future possibilities is essential for a financial exchange venture to be successful.

All of these complicated considerations can lead to a lot of stress. It is important that you check the cost of any protections you have. You can feel this feeling if you only do certain things. Since your feelings are the driving force behind your business, they will likely not be correct. When you buy stock, you must do so only for legitimate reasons. If you have control rights, you must also be able to predict how costs will perform. Be sure to consider the end goal before you put resources into any stock. Once you've considered all of the factors, it is important to have a suitable leave' system in place before you purchase any stock. It's also important that you execute it without delay.

Do your research on the nuts-and-bols of financial speculation.

Before starting your very first financial exchange venture or exchange, you should make sure that all of the essentials and protections are understood. The following areas are essential to know before you begin any securities trading exercises.

You should make it a priority to grow your securities exchange ventures.

It is possible to make a smart decision about how to differentiate your financial trading portfolio after you have conducted all the necessary research. You can also agree that you will be allowed to identify any potential threats, which could gently threaten your case. These two locations will allow you to sell securities exchange speculations prior to continuing any risky misfortune.

The main reason they do so is the assurance that every property will not be affected by an unexpected occurrence. It all boils down to the clear certainty that stock growth can help you quickly recuperate from the expulsion of a single or even a few speculations.

Here are the top 5 most common mistakes you should avoid

Securities exchange contributing can be a risky game, especially if the contributor isn't a skilled financial professional. Your capital could quickly dissolve if you aren't cautious.

1. Resource allocation to small organizations at the top.

Since I was a youngster, I have been selling and purchasing shares for quite some time. However, I am still amazed that so many new financial professionals put so much of their money into low-cost organizations trying to find the next five-bagger, ten bagger. They will visit different securities exchanges. They will be encouraged by the small organizations to sign up for these smaller groups that are likely to be the next huge thing. However, many of them will fail so it's mostly just betting.

One way to make your life easier is to focus on the reliable productive top organizations. And, ideally, only work with those who have a history of developing income and profits. After you have gained enough experience, it is possible to begin looking at ways to increase your portfolio by including a few smaller top organizations. You don't have to own a handful of high-chance assets in your portfolio. As long as the rest of your portfolio is comprised of more secure ventures.

2. A diverse portfolio.

This follows on from the previous point, that you should never spend too much. It is important to not invest all of your money in one or two organizations. You should also try to spread your risk among organizations. This could make you too exposed, which can adversely impact your portfolio. If the area or number of organizations that you put resources into goes down, it may also affect your portfolio.

3. Without utilizing a stop misfortune, putting resources into shares.

The most common mistake that untrained financial professionals make is not using a stop-misfortune. Although there may be disagreement over whether you don't need to bother with a stopping misfortune if you are contributing Warren Buffet style with a ten-year or multi-year viewpoint, the rule is that you should use a stopping misfortune to limit your troubles.

Northern Rock or any other UK bank is an example. These organizations would have reduced your ventures to almost nothing if they had been created a year or so ago. However, even if you had used stop loss of state 10% to 20%, your ventures would still be viable.

The most common error I see in financial professionals is to purchase stocks because they seem small. The value of a small stock is all that matters. It is one thing to have a 50-dollar stock and control one thousand dollars worth advantages. But it isn't the same as having a 100-dollar stock and 10 thousand dollars worth resources. The model was impossible to implement. But, let's face it, this is not the case.

The next most important error made by speculators is to link an organization with individual reasoning. These issues are not based on any monetary sense or expectation. Many people invest resources in organizations because they like the organization. This is an awful idea. You could put resources in an organisation just because you like it. The organization and its executives might not be what you desire, but other people could love it. A few people may also be dependent on useless diagram examples and volume. This is why they rarely work when they are used. Warren Buffett, among other prominent speculators, stated that viewing graph examples or volume leads to disarray and very rarely results in profit. These facts prove that only a handful of brokers have made a living off of specialized diagram designs. But, what number of them are able to reliably make a profit? What name do wealthy transient traders know?

If we can get past all the mental impediments that hold us back when we buy organizations, we can make more money and have a happier, more secure future. All of them are essential to purchasing and running great organizations and then securing their financial future.

The speculation scene is often exciting and rapidly developing. As the years go by, it is possible to learn a lot from those who take the time to study the key standards and the different resource classes. Understanding how to identify different ventures, and what each rung on the "hazard-stepping stool" is the first step.

Nugget

Contributing can be overwhelming for apprentices. There are many benefits to adding to a portfolio.

The venture 'hazard-stepping stool' recognizes resource class dependent on relative peril. Money is the most stable while elective speculations are the most unstable.

It is often the best thing for another financial professional to stay with assets on the list or to trade in funds that match the market.

Understanding the Investment Hazard Ladder

Here are the key resource classes on the venture-hazard stepping stone.

Money

The most convenient, cost-effective and safest venture resource is a money bank store. This store provides financial specialists with exact information about what premium they'll be purchasing. It also guarantees that they'll be able to recover their capital. There is one drawback: The premium from money held in a bank accounts only here and then beats expanding. The fundamentally fluid instrument of declarations of deposit (CDs) is money. However, CDs usually have higher loan fees than accounts. Cash is usually kept for a period of time, with possible early withdrawal penalties.

Bonds

A bond is an obligation document that refers to a loan made by a lender to a speculator. A run of the-mill security can be either a partnership (or an administration organization), where the borrower will pay the moneylender a fixed financing fee in return for their capital. They are used to back tasks, buys, etc.

Security rates will be determined by the loan cost. This is why they are often exchanged during quantitative facilitating, when the Federal Reserve or other national banks raise financing costs, and so on.

Stocks

Parts of stock allow financial experts to take an ownership interest in the organization's future success using increments in the stock cost and through profits. Investors may have a claim on the organization's benefits in the event of liquidation, which is when the organization fails. However, they don't enjoy the benefits. Holders of regular stock enjoy voting rights at investors' gatherings. Even though they don't have voting rights but enjoy the inclination to increase their profits, holders of favored stocks are eligible for more than ordinary investors.

Common Funds

A natural reserve is when more than one investor pools their money to buy protections. Portfolio directors supervise shared assets and designate and circulate them into stocks, bonds, protections, and other products. Individuals can put resources into shared assets as low as $1,000/share. This gives them the chance to differentiate into as many as 100 stocks within a portfolio.

Sometimes, shares assets are meant to replicate hidden lists such the S&P 500, or DOW Industrial Index. Portfolio directors keep track of the assets and make adjustments to them as necessary. These assets can have significant costs, such as front-end and yearly administration charges, which can be costly for financial professionals.

Shared assets are valued towards the end of each exchanging day. All sale and purchase exchanges are in the exact same manner after the market closes.

Exchange-Traded Funds

ETFs, or Exchange-Traded funds (ETFs), are very popular since their appearance in the mid-1990s. ETFs look like common assets. However, ETFs can be traded for the day as part of a stock trade. These prices reflect the buying and selling of stocks. It also means that their value may change drastically during an exchange day.

ETFs can use a hidden file to track stocks, such as the S&P 500. It can contain any combination of developing markets, items, single business areas, such as biotechnology and agribusiness. ETFs are well-known among financial professionals due to their ease of exchanging and broad inclusion.

ETFs are not the best investment option.

1. Being Late

Supporting is one of the most common mistakes. Most people support later. This is because speculators are quick to make sure their portfolios are secure after their positions have become troubled. A market pullback can lead to a higher price for security. Many will pay more to be safe.

2. For the right exposure, don't hedge

One common oversight when it comes to ETF support is that financial specialists fail to build a specific enough arrangement. This is because they want to be protected against the possibility of an unexpected hazard. To avoid making a mistake, you need to be careful not to confuse your exposures.

If your portfolio is made up primarily of little tops and you need to keep it secure, choose the right instrument.

The other is a growing lack of particularity.

3. Over-Hedging

There is ample evidence that long-term investing is possible. Long-term investing is possible if you are a long term financial specialist. Protecting your portfolio from any adjustment or other hazard can make you pay a high premium to get the protection you do not intend to use. To put it another way, you can cause more damage to the portfolio if your goal is to make sure it works rather than to leave it alone (make it a point to increase and rebalance).

Although it's understandable and necessary, you won't likely need to support for occasion danger unless you have exceptional strategic thinking.

Chapter 5: Guide To Swing Trading

"I have two fundamental rules that will help you win in trading as well in your life: (1) Do not bet. You cannot win. (2) If all your money is lost, you cannot bet.

Larry Hite

Many traders have found different trading methods that work for them and allow them to achieve their goals. Swing trading is popular among traders due to its flexibility. Instead of worrying that security will be available in a matter of minutes or hours you can have it for up to 24 hours and wait for the swing to happen.

Swing trading has recently become very popular. Swing trading is a popular choice for both professionals and beginners who want to place bets on market price movements to earn profit. Swing trading can be a rewarding hobby for professionals as they no longer have to stare at their computer screens all day.

Swing trading means that you trade in the markets for either a short or long term. This could be anything from a single day to several months. Swing traders spend lots of time looking at the market and studying trends. They wait for the price swing to take them to their profit by analyzing and continuing to analyze the direction of the market.

Swing trading sounds logical and simple on paper. But, your success in swing trading depends on many factors. You can't trade swings as actively as day trading. However, you have to stick to the rules to ensure your long-term success.

What is Swing Trading exactly?

Swing trading refers to the trading style of making profits in the stock market over a few days or weeks. Swing traders are not interested in holding a stock or other financial instrument for a prolonged period. The trader is looking to take a quick profit and then move on with the next swing trade.

Swing trading is a process that involves planning and following a schedule. This will help you plan your day and keep you on track. You should allow for preparation. This will allow you to spend time looking at stocks and analyzing them.

It is important that you understand that many institutional trader do not deal with swing traders. Their portfolio is large enough so that they don't have to hold onto their financial security for more than a few days. The vast majority of those who trade or buy financial instruments in the swing market are individuals who are managing their portfolio.

Knowing the basics of technical and fundamental analysis is key to success in swing trading. It is important to be familiar with how macroeconomic indicators and macroeconomic indicators can be used to set new prices. In order to validate trading decisions, technical analysis is combined with fundamental analysis.

The psychology of swing trading

Swing trading differs from day trading. A mental program is necessary to be able to successfully trade swings. Swing traders are not successful if they don't believe in you. Before you start swing trading, prepare your mind mentally.

The following mindset changes are necessary to achieve success with swing trading.

1. Long-term perspective

Instead of focusing only on one or two wins or losses per day you should focus on how many trades you place each week and how much profit you are hoping to earn. Another way to put it is to focus on the percentage of profit you hope to earn from your swing trading at each quarter's end. This is how progress can be measured.

2. Don't personalize your losses

Many traders become frustrated and hooked up with trading when the market goes against them. It is important to remain emotionally neutral when you lose and win. Bruce Kovner was right to say, "If I personalize my losses, I can't trade." If you want to make long-term swing trading profitable, you need learn from those losses and develop a trading system that will produce consistent success.

3. You should create a swing trading plan that you can stick with.

This is your key to success. To be successful in swing trading you must create a customized plan. If not, you will continue to feel emotionally unstable as you trade one after another. This is crucial if you wish to remain emotionally stable. Follow your plan if it is working. Success is very predictable. You should only make adjustments to your plan when the markets change.

Swing Trading: The Benefits & Risks

What are the pros/cons of swing trading and how can you avoid them? It is important to learn about swing trading. Without knowing the risks and benefits associated with swing trading, you are gambling. Winners are more likely to know the risks involved in their trade and can then plan a way to reduce them.

They trade without making the right adjustments necessary to maximize their trading success. This article explains the risk/reward of swing trading.

Benefits of swing trading

1. You trade faster

Swing trading requires less time than day trading. This is because swing trading allows you to place trades more often. It doesn't matter if you place one trade per day or one trade per week. It is also easy to forget about fluctuations in the market.

2. Short Term Profit

Swing trading is all about making short term profit by studying the market closely and making the most price changes. It might not be easy to make huge profits from price swings but it will pay off when you consider the cumulative gains over time.

3. Technical Analysis

Instead of worrying over fundamental indicators, technical indicators can be used to guide your buying and/or selling decisions. This will enable you to profit from any increase in price and profit.

Swing Trading Risks

1. Short Term risk

Swing trading has its challenges. You'll make short-term profits and also take on the short-term risk of market price changes. It is possible for financial instruments to fluctuate between high and low within days or weeks before they settle. These short term risks can occur when you trade swings. Here is where the technical and fundamental analysis come into play.

2. Market Changes Like Never Before

The market can't be controlled. You cannot control the market. Sometimes, the market can move against you despite your best efforts. It's best to not let this become your normal trading pattern. Unprecedented market changes can cause you to lose some of your capital.

3. Don't miss long-term trends

Swing trading is a way to make short term profit for a long time. Position traders focus on long-term patterns to make large profits. You will miss these long-term profit margins and trend opportunities.

Picking the Right Securities to Trade Swing

You can swing trade regardless of what plan you have. First, choose a trading market. Next, select financial security. You won't be able to make any progress if there is no way to know which market to trade stocks, bonds, the money market, options, or currencies. You should decide what kind of market to trade before you begin trading.

1. The Market Size

If you're interested in swing trading, there is a lot of stock options available: small, medium, and large. You need to know where you are. However, large-cap stocks can be very volatile and great for swing trading.

2. Volatile and sedate stock

In ideal situations, you will have the option to trade volatile stocks or those with enough market volatility to earn a profit. Trading on volatile stocks where there is enough market volatility to make a profit, or trading on stable stocks that move frequently, requires the technical indicators to confirm that trade. Remember that swing trading is about short term profits and minimizing market volatility. This will help you choose the right stocks.

3. Stocks with low prices and high price

What are you thinking about? What are you thinking? If this is your trading strategy, you can choose to make money from penny stocks. However, you should take into account several factors such as the trading volume, volatility, price history and price history before trading low-priced stock.

4. Bear & Bull Market

A bull market or bear markets are another indicators that can help you determine the best market for your trade. To determine which stock to trade, it is crucial to look at the market conditions. Before trading, be sure to examine the pattern of financial security.

Swing Trading: How to Find the Best Entry & Exit points

After you have decided on your security, and decided how much money you want to trade you must look for the opportunity. The timing and the opportunity are crucial in swing trading. You need to identify the exit and entry points that will most likely ensure a profit.

Because swing trading is short-term, it is important to use technical analysis to trade. Then you should pay attention to fundamental news. It is essential to understand and master the basic technical indicators used for swing trading. These are the indicators you should use and be vigilant for.

1. Simple Moving Averages (SMA)

2. Exponential moving average (EMA)

3. Support and resistance levels

4. The Fibonacci retracement

Moving Average for Small (EMA)

This is probably the most simple and robust technical indicator to use when swing trading. The analysis of the average daily prices for security stocks over a certain period of time can help to identify buy and sell signals.

A 10-day SMA (short for Stable Market Average) is calculated by taking the closing prices of the financial instruments over the last ten (10) calendar days and then multiplying it by ten ten (10). If the market is moving in one direction, the SMA helps you forecast the next range of prices.

A 20-day SMA will also be calculated in the exact same manner, except that the number of days will now be twenty (20), divided twenty (20). The next step after determining the average of moving averages is to plot the figures, and then join the lines with a smooth curve.

The buy signal will be established when the SMA (10-day) crosses the SMA (20-day). This is an indication of an uptrend. In the opposite direction, a buy signal will be given. It is important to understand that the market responds faster to price changes if it has a shorter moving average.

Exponential Moving Means

Both the exponential moving median (EMA), and the simple moving average are closely related. Only thing to be aware of is the slight variation in their calculation. Both are used in order to determine the buy and sell signals of a market.

The market trend can be determined by crossing two EMAs. This will allow you to forecast your exit strategy. The simplest of these is the 9, 13 or 50 exponential moving mean. It is a bullish sign if the price breaks of EMA occur above the starting level.

Generally speaking, a buy signals is triggered whenever your 9-day EMA crosses over the 13-day EMA. If your 13-day EMA crosses, or is above, the same thing will occur. These indicators can be considered a buy signal. You should still verify the fundamental news before you make a decision.

Conversely, a price break of the EMA below the start point is a sign a bearish or downward market. This is reflected by the 9day EMA exceeding the 13day EMA, and the

13day EMA being lower than or crossing below the 50day EMA. To make the right trading decision, it is important to look at the time frames of the bearish and bullish markets.

Support and Resistance Levels

You need to keep in mind that support level refers to the point at which the buying forces of a market outweigh the sellers when swing trading. This is when the underlying security's value drops, and a bearish market begins. You must purchase at the support bounce point and place your stoploss below it to profit from market changes.

The resistance level is on the opposite side. It is the area where the selling forces outweigh the buying. This causes financial instruments to fall below market value and creates a bullish marketplace that then reverses. This is a great opportunity to leverage swing trading. You must sell at the bounce level, and your stop loss should be above the resistance.

Fibonacci Retracement Patterns

Fibonacci Retracement is a pattern that can be used in order determine support or resistance triggers. This allows you to see when the price of financial instruments will reverse back to a specific level in order stabilize a trend. How can you determine the support and resistance levels for the swing trading market using Fibonacci Rectangle?

You should keep two Fibonacci ratios in mind: 23.6%, and 61.8% for reversal.

The price of the security's underlying security falls to the 61.8% Fibonacci level, then bounces back, and this indicates a resistance trigger. It sends the sign to enter and to buy. However, if the price of underlying security fluctuates above 23.6% Fibonacci and then falls back, this will signal a support level and a signal to sell or exit the market.

Swing Trading Profits

There are many factors that influence the amount of profit you make from swing trading, but the most important is your trader. The trader's trading plan, preparation, strategies as well as capital investment and the system all impact how much you earn per trader and over time. Most trades will earn you between 2% to 15% and compound the profits over time.

It also depends on the asset type you are trading. Some assets have higher yields and others are better. It is crucial to remain within your "circleof competency." You should be able to trade in the asset class you find most comfortable and make consistent profits with strategic trading.

After trading for a while, you'll be able to report your trading returns and profits. Keep track and keep track of all your earnings. This will allow you to make better financial projections, which will help improve your monetary trading insight.

Strategies to make Swing trading profitable

There are some things that you need to remember when you're swing trading. These tips will allow for you to minimize mistakes and increase profits over time. You must be focused, patient, and emotionally stable during your trading period.

1. Find the best swing trading broker

Your broker is more than your partner. It is important to select the right broker to help you succeed in swing trading. Analyze what your swing trading needs are and look for the type of trader that can best help you.

There are many brokers that target a particular market. If you want to succeed in swing trading, make sure you only choose brokers that are specialized in your trade niche. Demo accounts are available to test the platform and get a feel for how it works before you start trading. A portfolio of financial securities can be built to help you monitor the platform and trade in future.

2. Stay up-to-date with financial news in the market

Swing trading is a profession that requires you to keep up with financial news. If you are just jumping in and out of a market to see trends, you'll be out of business. Larry Hite said it best: "I have two simple rules for winning in trading, as well as life. (1) If you don't bet, then you can't win." (2) If all your chips are lost, you cannot bet.

You need to stay informed in order not to lose your place in the game. Listen to market information reports, commentaries and stock corrections. Also, read company reports, weekly charts, price trends, industry performance news, weekly charts, weekly charts and other reports. To make informed buying and selling swing-trading choices, it is essential to stay current with the market.

3. Get a learning edge

Learning is key to successful swing trading. If you want success in the market, you need to be focused and learn constantly. You should be able to learn from all markets and financial securities.

Paul Tudor Jones once said that "the secret to success from a trading perspective" is to have an unquenchable thirst and indefatigable thirst for knowledge and information. Use podcasts, videos tutorials, books and many other sources to keep learning.

Chapter 6: Start Soon, But Start Small

The longer we put off starting, the less we will get in return. This doesn't only affect the amount we save but also the potential interest our investments and savings could earn. Savings can grow a lot faster than money that you would normally save. It is never too late to start saving. Even if it's not your goal to retire at 65, you can still save money for a vacation or buying a home. While we should save for retirement, it is always better not to spend the money on pointless things.

This mentality of pushing back is what causes so many people to get into trouble. You will soon be approaching retirement, and may wonder where your money is coming from. It is not only about retirement. Perhaps you're in your thirties looking for ways to send your children to school or wondering if you can pay off student loans before you die. It is hard to be responsible. It is always more fun to buy a new bag, or keep up with your car upgrades. However, this is not the smartest thing to do. So that you can take better care of yourself in the future, you must start to think about how you treat yourself now.

We'll be disappointed if we take too many risks and begin too soon. If all $5,000 of savings is put towards one investment next Wednesday, and that investment doesn't succeed, you will feel disappointed and discouraged. You may even decide to stop investing. Instead, you should start small and invest less than 10% of what your savings are. It's easier to win if you keep things simple. Then you will find more success, which will provide you with the motivation and power needed to maintain a positive mindset. If you keep losing and risking, you will never be able to stop trying.

The riskier the investment, the more likely you are to lose. When you invest, you have to be open to taking risks. You will not always be able or able to take the same risks you desire.

At times, you may have to reconsider whether you should invest more in certain investments. It takes practice before you can achieve the right level of risk/return/loss. It is important to start small. Think of it as a runner. You would first start in the smaller races, before you try for the big one. Because you are aware that practice is key to becoming the best. Also, you know that failures will only make it harder to try again.

While it is important to be optimistic at the start, we need to also make sure we are being smart. It is important to have passion, enthusiasm, and a sense of hope in order to see the return on your investment. However, these emotions can be overwhelming.

There are two rules to this game. You must not lose money and compound interest.

Compound Interest

A compound interest is interest on the interest that already exists. There is an amount that your investment can earn, as well as an amount that you'll earn in interest. If you give your investments time, most likely your savings for a while, this will allow them to grow faster.

Your money earns you interest. You can earn interest by putting your money into a savings account. An interest amount will be earned if your retirement fund is included. This is also known as compound interest. It is the interest earned from that amount. This is something investors should remember to do.

It also earns more because it is just there. The principal's value grows with every dollar.

Example

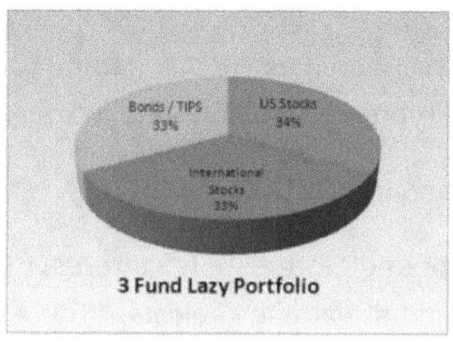

3 Fund Lazy Portfolio

It is important to assess if your investments are the right ones. You must ensure that you are earning the correct amount of compound interest in order to reach your goals. The formula to calculate this is:

A = 1 + r/n). (nt).

A is your compound income.

P is the principal sum.

r is your interest rate. For this, you would use an decimal.

N represents the number of times each year that interest is compounded.

nt refers to the time in years that the investment took.

Let's take a look at this example. Let's imagine that $7,000 is invested for ten year at a 5% interest rate.

The formula would then be A=7000 (1+.05/12) (12(10)).

In this scenario, the compound interest would amount to 11,529.07.

Don't Lose Money

It is essential that when we invest, we make sure we are actually making money and not just having a constant, steady flow. If inflation and investment are not compatible, there is no point in investing.

Compound interest and a return on investment must be considered. Sometimes, we are unaware that our money is not actually making money, but that the income is constant.

Example

This formula will help you make sure your money is going to make more from your investment.

You will want to make sure you actually gain money after a long period. You can use this formula for a quick estimate of how long it will take you to double your investment. This is also known as the Rule of 72.

The formula is 72/the Interest Rate.

It looks simple, and it really is. For example, if you invest $10,000 and get a 6% interest rate, it would take 72 years. You would need 12 years to convert $10,000 into $20,000.

When investing, you need to ask yourself if your investment is worth it. Although you would make just over $1,000 per year, if you work every week to earn that money, it is unlikely it will be worthwhile.

Chapter 7: What Is Network Marketing And How Does It Work?

Network marketing can be a viable option for those who are interested in a part time job or starting a small business. Network marketing is a great option for anyone looking to earn an income. There are no upfront capital investments. Sometimes you just need to purchase a product then sell it directly to someone.

Multi-level or network marketing is a business model which allows people to make money by either selling products or training new employees. The sales reps are the recruits. The downline is the group of reps that makes sales. They generate income from each sale or referral.

Network marketing involves a pyramid structure network consisting of individuals who sell the company's product. Participants in this network receive commissions. Each time they make a sale, or when their recruits do the same, they get a commission.

Participant will receive a commission each time they, or one of their fellow recruits in the network, make a sale.

It could also be defined as a direct sales strategy in which unemployed, independent people act as distributors of products. They must recruit additional sales reps to augment their staff.

This business model allows you to distribute any product. It has a negative history and is therefore restricted in certain countries.

Sometimes, a network marketing company might decide to reward participants who recruit others instead of for selling their products. A pyramid scheme could be a network marketing program that pays people solely for their recruitment. It is important to do your research before joining any network.

Network marketing is an excellent source of residual income if your personality includes being social and good at communicating. Residual revenue is money that you earn even after you sell your first product. The interest earned by one after investing in stocks is an example of residual income.

Consumable products such personal care, vitamins, and cosmetics are all good candidates for network marketing. Network marketing is a good fit since the reorders of these products create residual income which drives the network.

Your network marketing begins with your family members and friends.

Because network marketing is a form of bonus marketing, the commissions paid are usually lower because they are used to pay bonuses to higher up in the pyramid.

Because of the following reasons, it is very easy to draw people into network marketing:

It is cheaper to get started. This business model does require minimal capital investment. It takes only a product sampling and a distributor's kit to get your company off the ground. It doesn't take a lot of inventory to get your business started.

Network marketing allows for more people to participate. Multi-level market is a concept which involves both full-time or part-time employees. This allows those who are employed to join at a time that suits them, and also provides full-time employment for those who are unemployed.

- There's great potential for growth.

-

Characteristics of Network Marketing

* Independence. Participants in network marketing are known as independent business owners, since they promote products as if it were their own. There's also freedom in what and how you work.

* The Selling Philosophy. Participants will use the following marketing philosophy when selling. It's important to recruit as many

people and sell as much products as possible. Participants can even convince others to buy their products or join them.

* A big hierarchy. A person named X is going to have a person named Y. X will earn a commission each time he sells. He will also get a percentage of Y's sales commission. Y will need to search for W and Z to help him make more money. W and Z will pay him a share of their commissions for every sale, and so forth.

* No advertising. Companies selling through network marketing don't need advertising. This is because network marketing promotes their products through personal contacts that have more impact. This method allows them to persuade more people with their products.

* No fixed salaries. Participants in network-marketing are not employees. They do not earn salaries. They are paid commissions. The more you are successful in recruiting and selling, the higher your earnings.

* Accountability. Everyone is responsible for their actions. Your success will depend on your efforts. The more you sell, the more you will make.

* Direct sales. The network marketing method allows companies to sell directly their products. They do not have a clearly defined distribution channel and rely on the participants to help them distribute their products. Participants receive a commission each time they sell.

Online Network Marketing

The foundation of network marketing success is the formation of networks of people that deal with specific products. Therefore, the internet, which is home to billions upon billions, is a perfect place to create networks.

You have many benefits when you build your network marketing company online. You can work online from your home. It's possible to do it for everyone.

The first step towards building an online company is to get a domain. It is always recommended to use your personal identity (e.g., yourname.com). You can choose a name that highlights what you do, or search for something interesting. Try many different names before you settle on one.

Once you have the domain you can begin to build your site. If you don't know how to build a website, you might consider hiring a designer to do it or using a site builder. The following are essential features for your website:

- More information about your company or products.

- A system for ordering products.

- Details on training and information about the support system.

- The benefits of joining your business

- Users will receive a free eBook if they provide their email and names.

An autoresponder sends emails every person who contacts you.

If your website is functional, then you can start to market it. There are many marketing options available, including the creation of a blog, pay-per click advertising, email, and other forms of marketing. You want to draw as much traffic and choose the most effective strategy.

You can increase the likelihood that potential buyers will contact your company to purchase your product if you have a strong presentation online.

Tips to make your network marketing successful

* Use your judgment

You should carefully consider the following factors before you choose a company to work at. The company should be stable and offer products and services that customers are interested. Verify the company's pay plan and integrity. Also, make sure you are satisfied with their management. Make sure that the company has a system for training employees and a business system.

* Learn from a mentor.

You must be open to being guided by your mentor. Always be willing to listen. It is possible for you to copy the successes of your mentors. You should follow these systems.

* Evaluate the upline

The people in your company should be supportive. Are they invested in your success? Are they helping create a viable plan? Are they people you can reach at any hour of the night if you have questions? That company's support network is extremely important.

* Offer to help your downline

An "orphan" is a term used in this industry to denote someone who was brought into the world, but is now gone. Perhaps he's busy looking for others to bring in. Don't bring orphans to the company. Spend at least one month with them. Keep your hand on them and teach them until they can stand independently. You have to be willing and able.

* Use the internet:

Use the internet as a tool for marketing. Following up is crucial for any business. To maintain a relationship with your customer, you must contact them again after the initial contact. Autoresponders can be used to create websites if you choose the internet as your marketing medium. Autoresponders will help you follow up on leads when you get them.

* Be cautious with business:

This business is like any other. It doesn't make any difference if you run an electronic storefront. It's important that you take care. It is a good idea to have someone you can trust. A lawyer who is familiar with business laws may be a good option. You may also consider hiring an accountant to assist you with managing your accounts. You should do your research before you begin a business. This will help you understand the tax implications of the business.

* Do not rush to quit your fulltime job.

You shouldn't quit your day job until the company is right for you. Make sure you stay with the company and that it is stable. Last but not least, ensure that the income the company provides is equal to or exceeds your current income.

Network marketing pros

* Working remotely. Network marketing allows people to work from their homes, which many people would love.

* Network marketing can help you leverage your income. This allows you to make income from selling products. You don't have to make a living from it.

It is very easy to set it up. To start a network marketing business, you don't need to have much capital. It's a low-risk business that requires low capital investment.

Cons of Network Marketing:

* Many people don't become rich through network marketing.

* Less then 6% of sales take place online. The majority of sales take place face-to–face. Many people don't have the courage or confidence to talk to strangers.

* Growing your business takes time.

Chapter 8: Portfolio Building

After creating your investment portfolio you need to maintain it. This chapter will explain how to build on your portfolio.

How to build a passive portfolio and make good profits

Lazy portfolios are designed to be flexible and adaptable to market conditions. These portfolios are made up of small amounts of low-cost money that can be easily reevaluated and balanced. These funds are considered lazy because they allow investors to maintain the same asset allocation for longer periods of time.

Three portfolios with poor fund management

Three fund portfolios make up the majority of lazy portfolios. It consists of three categories of bonds: total American market, total global, and three bond types. Take into account that there are several close alternatives to these funds, particularly when purchasing them from Vanguards.

Source: Bogleheads

Core four portfolios

A portfolio can be created by combining core and extended assets. This is one of the most straightforward ways to create one. The core holdings comprise the bulk of a portfolio's risk- and return-features. The portfolio's final touches are completed by extended holdings. The core portfolio includes four different types, or 'cornerstones' of funds. The following chart shows how assets in core four portfolios are allocated.

Core-Four Portfolio and Asset Allocations within Core Four Portfolio

Desired

Stock/Bond

Allocation Vanguard Total

Bond Market

Index Fund Vanguard Total

Stock Market

Index Fund Vanguard Total

Stocks International

Index Fund Vanguard

REIT Index

Fund

60/40 40% 30% 24% 6%

80/20 20% 40% 32% 8%

Source: Bogleheads

Investing index ETFs can provide statistical advantages

ETFs are another option that can be an excellent investment. There are many options.

* Vanguard Total Stock Market eTF - It contains 34% of the stock portfolio. The Vanguard Total Stock Market ETF follows the

CRSP U.S. Total Stock Market. It covers all American stocks and has 19% of the total assets in medium sized businesses and 9% in those with smaller caps. Comparatively, only 12% of the S&P 500's assets are in mid-caps. There is no allocation to small funds. Stocks are typically weighted based on market value. This can be done by multiplying share prices with the number of shares outstanding. Apple currently holds 2.3% the total assets. The average market size of funds-related holdings is $37Billion. The funds currently pay 1.9% for expenses and 0.5% on an annual basis.

* Vanguard Total International Stock Index ETF. This ETF covers 22% the stock portfolio. It is reflected on the FTSE US Index with an average market capitalization of about $21 trillion. Fund assets are roughly 86% held by markets that have some development, with the remainder being held by emerging markets. Larger companies are more likely to take control of funds. About 17% is in mid-caps and 3% in smaller caps. The ETD

currently yields approximately 2.8% and charges around 0.14% on an annual basis.

* Vanguard Dividend Appreciation Fund ETF: It consists of 12% of the total stock portfolio. This index only invests in companies with a rise in dividends within the past ten-years. It follows the Nasdaq Dividend Achievers (which eliminates companies that have high levels of debt). Despite the emphasis on these dividends, it doesn't have a high yield. The S&P 500 has a similar 2.0% yield. While dividend appreciation may be considered an unusual index, the inclusion of it is due to increasing evidence that quality stocks, especially blue-chips with attractive dividends are performing well over time. Annual expenses also account for 0.1%.

* Vanguard Extended Market Index ETF includes 12% and follows the S&P Completion Index. It holds almost all tradable American public companies, not penny stocks, or any similar, that the S&P 500 doesn't currently own. The small caps have experienced an

average of 2.2% per year since 1926. This is much higher than companies with larger turnover levels but lower volatility. Currently, almost 6% of ETFs are invested in mid caps. Small caps also get 0.10% annual charges.

* Vanguard Emerging Markets Stock Index ETF – It includes 8%. This follows the FTSE Emerging Markets Index (850 stocks from 22 different developing countries). Since the end of 2011, emerging markets have been following US stocks less effectively than those in developed countries. However, this doesn't necessarily mean that rapidly growing economies shouldn't be considered in your long-term portfolio. The annual cost of this fund is currently 0.15%. Current assets comprise 30% of international stocks. The remaining 1/3 are from emerging markets. The annual return on investment portfolios over the last ten-year period, which ended in April 30, was 9.0%. The S&P 500 was able to return 7.7% per year over the exact same period.

The allocation of investment vehicles should be 70% to 75% for most investors. You should decrease this gradually as you get closer and closer to retirement. Many people will want to keep at most 50% of their investments in stock funds even after they reach retirement.

Chapter 9: Social Investing, What Is It?

Social engagement has attracted a lot more attention in recent years, especially after the financial crisis. Most people still wonder what social investment is. Let's look at this question. Let's ask this question.

First, let's look at how social investors view the environment in order to understand what social investment is. Creditors make decisions about investment options when conventional investing is done. They consider two things: financial gain and risk.

Price, return, and social effects Each participant has a certain level of confidence within the continuum. They invest within the continuum. An investor may be content to lose some of their return if a lower-cost investment is made. An investor might also gamble more if the return is higher.

Another aspect is financial participation-social consequences. Financial value is the way that investment-supported businesses support society over the profits they make for creditors. On the other hand, a business may have a negative impact upon society. When investing, a social investor also takes this into account.

Like conventional investors who are open to risk and reward, social investors are open to risk, reward, as well as social impacts. Social investors may, depending on their comfort, choose to forgo a financial return or take higher risks if the organization is trying to change the world.

Social investment simply means that you consider the impact on society when making investment decisions. This includes all investment strategies that fall within the scope of social investment. These include responsible investment.

Social screening: There are two major divisions within social investment: investment in effect or social screening. A social screener is an investor who has a list or social standards to meet.

Investor removes all companies that don't comply with the standards and invests in those "socially-responsible" companies that do so in a way that meets the investor's return and risks.

Many socially conscious mutual money have adapted this strategy. They start by screening for social issues, then identify an investment package that meets those criteria. Finally, they invest their management companies in the basket to reach the mutual funds' financial goals.

Impact investing - Also known as community or impact investment, this second category of social capital is called impact investment. Impact investing is done in businesses that provide social benefit and not in corporations doing no harm.

Under the effect heading "Investment offer programs" organizations are protected if they have a charitable or social purpose and also a corporate structure capable of producing profit and promoting capital spending. They are open to both industry and charity.

Non-profit and profit-making effect investment firms are possible to be established, but they are rarely listed on financial market as large public companies. Therefore, it is more difficult for an impact transaction to be made. This typically takes the form or private investment as a bill, loan, or even a loan.

Effect Finance Markets: What do these investment agencies have in common? Let's take a look at specific industries that are considered to be influence investments, in order for us to get a better idea.

Accessible housing has become a priority for most people. Habitat for Mankind isn't funded by most people. Charity, for instance, can fund Habitat by offering a low-interest loan for the organization to finance its programs.

Another side effect of funding are microfinance. A micro-finance organisation offers small loans to people in developing countries who want to set up or expand their businesses, and help them get out from poverty. A microfinance bank-like institution can produce profits and help investors.

Many related industries also raise income and have social missions: fair trade. Due to the social impact of these organizations on society, donors are also available to businesses in each market. They can give up some of their financial returns or take on more risk.

What is an Investment, and What Is a Social Investment Network (or Network)?

Speculation can be defined as an expectation that the future will produce a profit. This could include buying currency pairs, inventories or goods in the current world.

An independent decision is required to reach a judgment. This takes into consideration all information and determines the correct trade. Social trading involves the exchange of information. This allows for traders to make better decisions by copying and watching other traders. A single decision can lead to a decision.

Another way to invest in social investment networks is to copy the top performer of a social network, or to choose a trader who's doing well at the moment. social investment network

A network to promote social investment is a group that trades currency pairs between investors, inventories commodities or indices. Individual trading or copying positions are also possible.

Recent years have seen network trading rise. Social trading, which includes CFD trading in commodities and currencies as well as indices, is another form of CFD trade. Social trading involves copying other traders' positions and must be imitative. In other words, each trader will be able to see how other companies operate and how efficient they are on the markets.

One of the most prominent social trading companies in the world disclosed last month that they had received more than 50,000,000 trades in six years. According to them, 32 million of these transactions were duplicate trades. This means that 64% of the positions on their trading platform had been replicated by another investor.

A social trading network offers traders the opportunity to view other traders' positions and open positions. It is possible to observe how different currency pairs fluctuate, and how to reach the exchange.

Social trading, if your goal is to exchange and trade CFDs and spend money, may be a good choice. You should consider the potential benefits as well as risks associated with trading and investing CFD. Social investment networks often have a fixed amount per copy business. This reduces risk and allows users to diversify their investments.

Social Investment Fund

Social investment funds, also known as social investment funds, are grants that are provided in developed economies to support the needs of the most vulnerable. They can be used for small-scale social programs. The multilateral agencies' concern with indigenous poverty is relatively new. It can also be said that the issue originated in two different areas. The first is to explain bank-funded programs' effect on electricity, transport, integrated rural development, and other areas. It was a significant problem for banks, both in the past or today. Second, rural production. This was an area that primarily focused on the growth of non-indigenous farmers and their interaction with indigenous farmers. These programs are not designed to address socio-cultural concerns and do not focus on any one ethnic group.

Even though integrated rural development doesn't hold the old position as a viable paradigm, there is no new model of rural development. Most similar models are sustainable development projects, which place more emphasis on managing natural resources. Such programs can be used by both indigenous and other peoples to produce productive elements.

The schemes are targeted at rural poverty, in a context that is devoid of economic growth programs via social investment programs, education and healthcare programs, or microenterprises. The original purpose of micro-enterprises or social investment funds was not to combat rural poverty.

For small- and short-term loans, microenterprise lenders have been established in metropolitan areas. They offer low-interest rates that are lower than the consumer's. This money was invested in small-scale industrial, utility, or production activities.

The purpose of the first social investment funds was to reduce economic growth policies' impact. The Fund for Social

Emergencies, which was founded in Bolivia in 1986, was its first creation. It was designed mainly to develop jobs. The aim was to provide jobs for employees who had been laid off by the privatization at COMIBOL (state-owned mining company). Although the focus was more on infrastructure investments, almost all of the interventions were considered to be transitional measures until stabilization policies allowed for economic growth. Even though most of these social investments funds didn't have a significant impact on jobs they were still introduced in all Latin American countries and are now widely used in the developing countries.

Guide to Socially Responsible Investors

SOCIAL INVESTITIVE: What does that mean?

Socially Responsible Investment ("SRI") invests in order to increase the returns on investments, but also in pursuit of social welfare.

Socially conscious investing was first developed during plantation business in the mid-1700s. Investors were initially persuaded not by the company but eventually joined religious institutions to warn them against "sinful" businesses that produce weapons, liquors, cigarettes.

Socially responsible investment was established in the 1960s to account for greater social concerns, such as women's equality, civil and working rights, and other environmental and social issues, such as South Africa's apartheid in 1970s.

SRI has slowly adopted the larger field of constructive developments within the environment, Social Justice and Corporate Governance since the 1990s. I use the SRI title, however, as it is still commonly accepted as such. SRI assets exceeded $3 trillion in early 2010, a 380.0% increase relative to $639 Billion in 1995, which was the date of the initial Social Investment Forum study.

SRI assets have grown 34% in 2005, while assets previously controlled by the government only increased by 3.3%. The difference between traditional assets professionally managed and those of SRI assets was a decrease of 1% from 2007 to 2010 (during recession), compared with a 13% increase. Today, more than one-eighth of every eight dollars goes to socially responsible spending.

Social Investment Forum attributes most of the growth to customer demands, legislation, and regulation in an a smaller way.

Approaches to Investing There are three investment strategies that can be described as SRI. Positive/negative screening: aggressive screening requires the identification of healthy firms. This helps companies choose businesses that can be based on their business operations. Investors might choose to invest in the solar industry if they are particularly concerned about environmental sustainability.

Many people think that investing money in businesses that support environmental or social causes will result in sacrificing efficiency. However the truth is, this seems to be false in practice. Marc J. Lane, the author and co-author of Successful Socially Conscious Investing discovered that the best businesses have higher financial performance. Lane says that the stock prices of these companies surpassed those of the Russell 3000 Indices for 8 years.

Negative screening is, exactly, what the name implies: Businesses whose business policies or products are not socially compatible. SRI participants include tobacco, firearms and gambling. The program has been extended to companies where the management is not able to encourage equity, fairness and organizational accountability to their workers.

Shareholder advocacy or shareholder advocacy. Shareholder activism is the attempt to influence changes in corporate policy and procedures. It involves presenting shareholder proposals that have been voted on by shareholders. In the initial instance of shareholder advocacy, less than 20 shareholder proposals were accepted each year. Social Investment Forum estimates more than 200 institutions had submitted their shareholder proposals in 2008 and 2010 and that all have been accepted.

Community Lending Financial funding is direct capital spending through participating lenders (also known as "Community Development Financial Institutions" and "CDFIs) for under-served members of government programs. These borrowers are eligible for insurance, equity, liquidity and other benefits that would not be available to companies or individuals if they applied for loans from commercial banks. Venture capital funding will also support public assistance.

Directly investing in the community will make an investor more likely to have a greater effect on social good. While purchasing stock in companies may not lead to social gains but money invested in CDFIs, risk management funds or other financial instruments can be used specifically to support the needs of underserved people.

SRI PRODUCTS MUTUAL FUNDS and EXCHANGE TRAADE FUNDS(ETFs).

There have been more than 250 mutual fund establishments, primarily for saving money that is in line with other social principles. Some reciprocal investment funds only focus on SRI businesses like Calvert or Domini, PAX World. Ariel, Sentinel and Winslow are some examples. Many reciprocal funds, including Vanguard, Neuberger Bernman, Gabelli or Legg Mason, offer one or more investment products that address social concerns.

Mutual funds offer a way to invest in different companies that have certain social values. But, before investing they must be limited.

Mutual funds are expensive. Many mutual funds companies charge continual fees, as well as charges for selling and buying shares.

Mutual funds, which are conservative forms of investing in SRI, have no control over the firm collection. You may be surprised at how many mutual fund companies invest in socially conscious business ventures.

Last but not least, mutual funds cannot solve a simple, static commodity like ETFs. The FTSE KLD 400 is one of the earliest SRI indexes. It was created in 1990. It had a positive result with 9.51 percent, compared with 8.66 percent in that same period starting December 31, 2009. ETFs that track FTSEKLD400 can be easily purchased at a fraction compared to mutual funds. They will perform just as well if they are not too expensive.

There are 26 eligible ETFs at the moment. Although they represent only 1% of the total SRI fund holdings, their holdings have grown by 225% in the past seven years, the fastest growth of any recorded investment.

STOCKS and BONDS There are two ways to invest in a socially conscious organization.

One is by directly investing in the stock or bonds of financially stable, sound companies that rely on your values.

It is often believed that you increase the risk of investing in shares in particular companies if you decrease the number or assets you invest. This can only happen if you are not performing work and invest only in companies that have low ethical, political, or social standards.

A number of publications have annual lists that list the best SRI companies. These are great places to start your search. ETFs can be an excellent alternative if you don't have the time to analyze or aren't interested in doing so. Another option is to subscribe to New Paradigm Capital twice a month, which provides you with investing ideas, trends, companies and companies to check out.

Alternative investing may include hedge funds, venture capital, private equity, land, and other unregistered partnerships or limited liability corporations. They are generally only available to highly qualified individuals with high net-value. This means that only a few wealthy people can invest in investments that have a $50,000 minimum investment.

This is not a simple matter. Hedge funds employ investors. They have the ability buy and sale by investment technology. These techniques are sometimes prohibited or inaccessible by mutual fund managers.

In general, increased resilience is associated with higher returns and greater ability to adapt to specific market dynamics.

Due to increasing investment in clean technologies, the SRI sector's controlled assets has increased by 610% since 2008.

Community Development Financial Institutions, or CDFIs, are:

Community development banks, credit associations for community development, community loan funds, and community venture capital funding are all examples of community development bank. All of these are forms of the lender and make capital available for individuals and small businesses in under-served neighborhoods.

Since 2007, assets of community-based banks have grown more than 60%.

Many of these institutions today reach their target customers online. Kiva.org provides microloans to entrepreneurs from developing regions of the globe. The repayment rate for the loan is 98.99 percent. However, the interest rates vary and are more favorable than the government's deposit rate.

GLOBAL Developments Several global developments will encourage investment in SRI.

Particularly, green investment in clean technologies, renewable energy and other forms of investment was a dominant issue in 2011. This resulted in increased SRI investment, particularly in alternative SRI investments such as hedge funds and private investment.

It's worth taking a step back from all the possible investment vehicles in order to see the whole picture. This will help you make sound decisions about where to invest your money. What are the top trends in innovation across industries, and especially in fields such as social responsibility?

Where can you go from HERE?

New Paradigm Wealth expects weekly news and a bimonthly Newsletter to guide investors with practical SRI choices right now. I also provided links to websites that help investors make smart investments and be socially conscious.

Now is the best time to align your investment principles with your convictions, prioritizes, and expectations.

Chapter 10: The Process Of Moving In

A residential property manager's top priority should be making the renting process as easy and as painless as possible. Not only for yourself, but for potential tenants, too. In this chapter I'll discuss the steps you can take to make your tenant's move-in process as easy as possible.

How to draft a Tenancy Lease Agreement

A tenancy agreement, or rental agreement, is an important legal document that sets out the roles and responsibilities for both the tenant as well as the property owner over the course of the tenancy. Before you move in, make sure all tenants sign a rental agreement. This will help to prevent any unpleasant tenants from becoming your landlord. Here is an example lease agreement.

Types and types of lease agreements

There are two types generally of lease agreements: the fixed-term and the automatic.

* Fixed-term lease

This allows the property owner to rent out the property for a set period. The tenant might sign a 2-year fixed term lease that starts in January 2021 and ends in January 20, 2023. Once the tenant has signed the agreement, they must pay rent for the entire term. This gives landlords peace of mind, as they don't have the responsibility to search for tenants until the lease expires. The landlord is assured of a steady stream of income.

It is important that you note that a fixed-term lease does not permit property managers to make any changes. It is not possible to increase or terminate the rent. In case the tenant wants to vacate the property, they don't have to give notice letters. The property owner will require the tenant to pay the entire rent until the tenant finds another tenant.

But this type of lease doesn't have to be final. The lease agreement can be ended by either party if certain conditions are not met. The landlord can end the lease if the tenant is not paying rent on time. However, a tenant could end the lease if he or she fails to make repairs to the property.

* Automatic leasing

This is a lease that is renewed every other month. It can be renewed monthly, biannually, annually, or any other time that suits the property owner. This agreement can be amended by the property owner at any time. They can also expel tenants if they provide a notice of at least 30 days (in most cases). If they want to vacate their property, the tenant must give notice (typically one month).

Let us now cover some of the key issues you should include in a residential lease agreement.

* Names of all Tenants/Occupants

When you draft a tenancy contract, make sure all tenants and their occupants (married and unmarried) sign it. This gives you additional insurance because each tenant must pay the full rental amount. This document also allows you to terminate the tenancy or evict all occupants if the tenants fail to follow the agreement and comply with their rental obligations.

* Description of Property

The tenancy agreement should detail all information regarding the property being rented out. It should include the address, house numbers, as well specific amenities such parking spaces and storage spaces that tenants are allowed to use. Be sure to include any areas that aren't allowed for tenants.

* Rent Price

This might seem like an obvious thing, but it's vital that you clearly indicate the rental cost for your property in the rental agreement. This is not all. You must also indicate the acceptable payment methods and the payment dates you expect your tenants follow in order for there to be no confusion.

* Maintenance and Repair Policies

It is essential that you are clear about your maintenance and repair policies in any rental agreement. This will help protect you from future rent withholding problems. This includes the obligation of tenants to maintain the property in a clean condition and to pay the damages incurred during the tenancy.

* Rules and Residency Policy

If there are rules you feel are so important that you would have to expel a tenant if they broke them, then it is important that you include them in your rental contract or lease agreement. Here are some of the policies you might consider including in your tenancy contract.

i. Smoking

As property manager, you can ban or restrict smoking at your property. It doesn't matter if you ban smoking on your premises. This also applies to vaping and other forms of marijuana smoking. You can also restrict smoking in your premises, but not ban it. In this case, you must mention where and what the tenants can smoke.

ii) Illegal Activities

To protect your tenants and property from damage, you should have a clause in the tenancy agreement that defines the criminal and disruptive acts that can be prohibited on your property. This includes drug use and sales, excessive noise and nuisance.

iii. Animals

With the exception for emotional and service support animals, pets are allowed or prohibited on your residential property. It is important to clearly state in the agreement whether your residential property allows pets. You should also mention what kind of pets you allow, how many pets the tenant can keep, and how big they are.

* Contact Details

Your renters can contact you for various reasons throughout the term of their tenancy. While text messages and phone calls can be acceptable in most instances, it might be more efficient and practical to communicate with renters through writing. This gives you a permanent record of your communications, which you can use to refer back to later in a legal case. Therefore, you should also share your email addresses and physical addresses with others so that they can contact you when necessary.

Questions to address before a tenant moves in

Now that you have finished the tenant screening, you have found a fantastic tenant to rent out your home. You are excited about your new tenant moving in. The possibility of earning some income each month now seems like a sure thing. You feel proud, and rightly.

It's a huge accomplishment to find a tenant who will take over the vacant space in your home. Finding a good tenant can be difficult, especially when we live in volatile economic times.

But, getting a tenant is just the first step. For your tenant to enjoy a great experience, it is essential to build a relationship with them from the beginning. Let's look at some of these steps to prepare your property and make it ready for an incoming tenant.

* Conduct final Health and Safety Inspections

A thorough safety and health assessment is the first step in preparing your residential home for a tenant. In order to protect your new tenants from potential liabilities and to prevent them from becoming liable, you must promptly address any health hazards. It could be anything, from loose handrails to faulty electric sockets that emit smoke when they are plugged in. Check under the sink as well to make sure that the plumbing isn't leaking. Leakage can cause water wastage and mold growth.

Furthermore, it is a good idea to get an electrical and gas certificate from professionals. This would protect you from any potential lawsuits or losses.

* Utility Systems

Next, make sure you check that all the utilities systems are in good working order. This includes electrical, heating, plumbing. All utilities are intended to make your property habitable. Therefore, tenants cannot move into your property if they are not working properly. You need to make sure that your heating and electricity are working correctly. It is important to check the plumbing for leaks, and get them fixed as soon as possible.

Verify that all water faucets are functioning and that there are no clogs.

* Lease Agreement

Once everything has been verified and the property is clean, it's time to review the rental contract and get the incoming tenant signed. As this will give you the opportunity to discuss your expectations, responsibilities and how you can best work together, it is a good idea to have a face-to-face review of the agreement with your tenant. By doing this, you can have a general idea of each others' expectations and responsibilities, which can help avoid conflicts later. To avoid future disputes, it is highly recommended you review each issue thoroughly. It is important to remember that esignatures are increasingly popular in today's digital age. Consider the possibility of signing your documents online.

* Deposit Payment and Rent

Once your tenancy agreement was in force, you will be eligible to collect your deposit and rent. The amount of the deposit you can collect on a tenant will vary between states. Arizona has a limit of one-and a-half times the rent while California allows for up to twice that amount. It is important to find out the laws in your state regarding deposit collection to ensure you comply with them.

This is one of the leading causes of landlord-tenant conflict. This issue is a sensitive one and you could end up getting sued. You should consult an expert in this field to learn more about the laws of your state regarding security deposits. This will save you money and prevent costly mistakes.

* Inspections

Before you let your tenant move in, make sure that the property is inspected by the required body in your state. This will ensure that the building meets all applicable codes and standards. You must immediately rectify any violations of safety and health standards and schedule another inspection if necessary. If you are unsure if your property should be inspected, contact us in advance to determine and take action.

* Contact Details

Last but not least, make sure you give your incoming tenants your contact information. Include your email address, phone number, and email address. This will allow them to reach you anytime they need. You are responsible for being available 24/7 to your tenants so you can respond quickly to any issues related to their residency. It is fine to set boundaries about when your tenants may contact you. Your tenant should know that you do not like to be bothered after 10.00 pm. If you have to respond to an emergency situation, it is important that you are available 24/7 to assist your tenants. This will help you instill trust and confidence in tenants as well as ensure they have a pleasant experience during their entire stay.

Ideas for welcoming a new tenant to your residential property

Tenants often find it stressful and challenging to move into a new house. There will be many things that tenants worry about. Is it possible to pack everything? Is it possible for the movers to arrive on time? What kind of neighbors can we expect? These are questions that may be asking your incoming tenant, and can make them feel nervous or uneasy. There are several things you can do, as a property owner, to make the transition as smooth and easy as possible. Let's take a look at some of the best ways to welcome tenants into your property.

* Provide them with information about utilities

It is always a good idea that you give utility information to your tenant, including the contact details of utility companies at least a week prior to them moving in. This is vital for two main reasons. First, it allows tenants to call utility companies to confirm that all utilities are working by the time they move into their home. It's not something you want to see your tenants move into a home only to discover that the gas has stopped working or that the heating system has stopped working. Your tenants can also contact the utility companies to make their utility payments and get their billing information.

* Provide Parking Information

If you rent a car to your tenant, it is important that they have details about the best places to park on your property. To be able to park on major streets, your tenant may have to register their car and get a sticker allowing them to park in designated areas. Your tenant's guests may need information to park in your property. Make sure they are informed.

* Provide a welcome package for them

For new tenants, moving into a new house is a stressful experience. You can leave a lasting impression with your tenants by offering a small and inexpensive welcome package. It is possible to establish a strong relationship with your tenants by showing them that you are more than clients. You could include these items in your welcome package:

* A few bottles of water to put in their fridge

* A few toilet paper rolls

* A few rolls for paper towels

* A multipurpose cleaning product in a glass bottle

It is a great way to build their trust and establish good relations during their tenure.

* Provide them with Keys, Openers and Other Codes

It is crucial that you ensure that your tenant moves in to your property with all the necessary keys. To avoid any potential problems with locking your tenant out, make sure you give them copies of each key.

* Provide Friendly Guidance to the Neighborhood

When moving into a home, it can be difficult to adapt to a different neighborhood. It can be daunting for some to be unfamiliar with the local people, as they don't know how others will react. It is possible to ease the worry by giving them some helpful tips on how they can navigate the neighborhood. Provide them with information about the closest grocery stores and convenience stores. A formal introduction can be made to your neighbor if your property has more than one tenant.

This allows you to have a positive personal relationship and build trust with your new tenant. It is vital to have a strong relationship with your tenant.

These easy-to-follow tips will make it easier for tenants to move in.

This chapter has its main points. Let us now recap: Here are some key points to remember when you prepare your property so that new tenants can move in.

* Write a comprehensive rental/lease agreement outlining your expectations as well as your responsibilities during the entire term of the tenancy.

* Make sure you review the tenancy agreement before your tenant moves in.

* Perform any necessary repairs and clean-ups before the renter moves.

* Ask for an official inspection by the relevant authorities. This will ensure that all safety regulations have been met and that your property remains habitable.

To avoid any problems, you must give the keys to all locks to your tenant before they move in.

* Prepare a welcome package to help your tenant feel at home upon their move-in.

* Make sure to introduce your tenant to their immediate neighbors (at their option of course). This will help them get to know each other.

Chapter 11: Set Your Personal Finance Principles

If you are struggling to make ends meet, it is not the best idea to invest your money in the stock market. Before investing your money, it is a good idea to get out of debt. We'll be discussing how to manage money so you don't lose all your investment capital. Let's get started with your basics needs.

Take care of your basics

Your basic needs should be taken seriously. If your family is struggling to provide food for their families, then investing your money should not be an issue.

In order to pay for your basic necessities, you need to find a job with enough money. You need to allocate some of your income for the essential expenses such as your food budget or your rent/mortgage.

Efficiency is key to being a good investor. Be efficient with your money management and let go of any recurring expenses you do not use. Consider switching to a cheaper plan if your cellphone bills are too high. To save money, you can cook your own meals if you do not buy ready-to-eat food. These are just a few easy ways you can save money.

Two prerequisites to investing are debt repayment and emergency fund savings.

Your debts must be paid

If you don't address financial obligations that accrue interest as soon as possible, it will affect your net worth. The bigger your debts get, the longer they are left unpaid. Before you can invest in the future, you must deal with your debts.

It is a good idea if you have debts to allocate a percentage of your savings to debt payments. If you've borrowed money from other sources, pay off the ones that have the highest interest rates. These debts are likely to grow faster than the rest and you should pay them off as soon as they are minimal.

Only invest if you are completely free of debts.

Once you've paid your debt off, it's best to avoid taking on more debts. This means you should not buy anything that will require you to borrow money. If you are required to borrow money in order to buy something, it is likely that you cannot afford it.

A credit card makes it much easier to accumulate more debt. Today it's almost impossible to avoid using your credit cards for everyday purchases. Keep your credit card spending in check by paying them on time each month to prevent it from growing. By setting up your bank so that it automatically deposits a payment for your credit card company, you can do this.

Set up an emergency fund

If you don't owe any debts, your savings can go towards your emergency fund. Your emergency fund is a money reserve that you can use in an emergency. This covers hospitalization expenses, legal costs, and emergency purchases.

Your emergency fund protects you and your assets in case of an emergency. It will help you deal with any misfortunes that arise without having to take out a loan.

Your emergency fund should not exceed six times your monthly expenses. Many people feel that this amount is excessive. In the event that your income suddenly stops, it is better to have enough money. In the event that you lose all your income, for instance, you will still have enough money to get you a job within six months. You will never be forced to accept a job you don't desire by having an emergency plan.

It is also crucial to replenish your emergency funds when you use them. If you make sure that your emergency fund remains full, you'll always be ready in case of an emergency.

Be strategic in your financial goals

Now that you have paid off your debts and saved money for any emergencies, let's talk about how investing can help us reach our goals faster. There are two basic types of financial goals. Short term and long term.

Savings for your short-term goals

There are certain types of goals you won't be allowed to invest in. It is generally not a good decision to invest money that is intended for a shorter term goal. It is unlikely that you will be able to recover your investment if there is an unforeseen circumstance.

Saving for these short term goals is best done the traditional way. These funds can be put in bank accounts with high interest rates. These funds will still grow during the time they are stored. Time deposits and savings accounts are two examples of bank products that can help you earn interest while avoiding market risk.

This strategy works best if you have goals that last less than 2 years. Avoid investing in stocks if you are not planning to use the savings fund within 2 years.

Invest for long-term goals

The stock market is more suited for goals that you can meet in the next 2 years. In order to maximize the value your goal funds, which you will use in 5-7 year time frames, it is a good idea to do this.

This type of goal will make your money last a long time. You can put your money to use by investing it in the stockmarket, even if your money is sitting idle.

sinvesting. You don't have to buy stocks with high returns. Instead, you can still take safer routes to achieve your goals.

If you need to grow your money quickly, you could be taking on more risk. You may have to invest in companies that are not familiar with your industry. You might be tempted to leave your money in a place you don't want.

Most importantly, you can make amends for mistakes if you invest for long-term goals. It is possible that your entire portfolio may have lost between 35-40% if it was sold to the market in 2007. If you were investing only for a very short term goal, there would not have been enough time to recover the losses. You might have some time to recover your investment if your financial goals are still distant. Keep your funds in a market for 3 to 5 years.

Chapter 12: Expert Trading Options

It will be much easier to trade in the foreign and domestic markets after spending time. You won't have to do as much work to find the next commodity in sharply rising value or to convert currencies. You will learn this as soon as you attain professional status and trade like you would any other profession.

What next is the biggest challenge for anyone trading on the open stock market?

What keeps things from becoming boring or monotonous?

First, there's always something new to learn in the forex markets. You never know what you might discover when you awake in the morning. There are several ways that you can profit from the differences in currency conversions and the time delay between markets which can affect trading value.

Arbitrage

You can trade certain commodities in multiple currencies in different markets on Forex. Even though computers have made global communication fast, the markets can still trade together with nearly equal securities values in all currencies.

This system is not perfect. It's possible for the value to rise or fall in one currency and country before it reaches another. The process of arbitrage, which is used by experienced traders to exploit delays in market development, has been used successfully by traders.

This is a transaction in which you purchase a stock or security at a lower market price while simultaneously selling it on a more valuable market. This process can be complicated so we'll use an example.

Let us suppose that one U.S. penny is equivalent to 0.5 British pound. All goods in British Pounds are twice as expensive simply because they have a numerical value.

Let us now consider the price for a share traded on each market. If they were equal, the stock could trade for two dollars in America and one pound at home. The time difference means that if anything happens, the stock value in the United Kingdom will drop six hours earlier than it would in the United States. This drop might not reach the American market immediately.

If the stock price falls below 0.8 pounds in the UK, then the purchase price in dollars is less due to currency translation. This would result in an arbitrage, where you could sell the stock in dollars that you bought in UK. By doing this, you were able to take advantage of the slow pass-through in the stock's loss.

Currency translation volatility

Trading based upon the changing rates is another way to capitalize on the ever-changing currency value. What does this actually mean?

The changing con-version rates are something you need to be aware of. If a currency exchangerate changes significantly, it's time to act. It is very similar in nature to arbitrage but is more risky due high volatility.

As an example, let's say you bought a stock on the U.S. exchange for $2 per share. But suddenly the British Pound gains in value and falls to half of what it was worth for two dollars. In this case, you would sell your shares to the British market. Because the value of a British pound is greater and has greater buying power,

However, it is best to have your foreign currency liquid assets immediately. This usually happens the same day. This is "tomorrow" as it takes two to three days for foreign currency delivery. Exchange the currency for share value on the same day and you will not have to wait to receive it.

Chapter 13: Alternative Trading Options

You don't have to be an expert in order to make money on stock markets. There are many ways you can make money. These options are worth exploring if your goal is to make trading stocks and shares a career.

Some types of trading require a lot of courage and determination. You are more likely to make a bad investment or suffer a substantial loss than you are with conventional trading strategies.

Day trading

Day traders have one of the highest market risks. Day traders deal with investments that are subject to rapid changes and can be lost or gained quickly. Day trading these stocks can cause huge volatility, so it is easy to lose a lot. It is very difficult to make large amounts of money in this field.

Additionally, these daytrade stock options can be extremely unpredictable. The so-called "overnight situation" is not a guarantee of what stockbroker/daytraders will open their doors the next day.

Forex has very little room for day trading as the market is constantly changing throughout the week. These cases require that day traders set a time limit before he exits and then sell all stock. This allows him to rest peacefully as the world continues to turn and gives him the opportunity to start the next day fresh.

Day trading is dangerous and not recommended to novices. Day trading has high risks. The risk of losing your money is higher for those with less experience than conventional trading. The majority of people who trade in this volatile area of the market have extensive trading experience. Before investing in this area of the market, traders carefully evaluate the risks.

Secondary markets

Secondary markets can be interesting because they are created for redistribution of money used to make loans. Fannie Mae (Freddie Mac) and Freddie Mac, two large companies, are two examples of secondary markets from which shares can be purchased.

Here's how it works. When someone purchases a house, they apply for a loan from the bank. The amount is usually around eighty percent of the total cost. This is granted. The bank then purchases the house and begins paying the monthly loan back to the bank.

Fannie Mac and Freddie Mac were created by the United States to buy mortgage loans from banks. So the bank gets the money back for future use.

What are these agencies to do with the deficit? They will sell it. They sell it on the secondary market. They mature at some point, which is likely to be around the same moment as the original loan. The investors then reap the benefits of the investment, with the income from the interest.

You can also profit from volatile stock markets by using a "swap", which is a way to take advantage of them. Swapping securities and bonds can be used to obtain lower interest rates. One example is that a U.K. company owns one security and a Japan company owns another. These commodities can be traded or bought to each other to reduce interest rates.

Consider a company that owns bond "A" paying only two percent interest on the current market. A different company holds bonds "B", which pay three percent interest, in its local market. Bond A is three percent and Bond B four percent in the foreign market. Both can make more money by bond traders. Both can benefit from each other selling securities because they both earn higher interest.

Swaps are not likely to be in your immediate future if this is confusing. It is more likely that this will be transacted between companies on the foreign markets than between individuals. However, it could be possible with the right broker. But, if you're able to complete the deal, all you need is to expect a higher margin and your broker will take over the rest.

If you decide to have stock options for your business, you'll likely hire a fulltime advisor to handle all your financial needs. This includes managing your stock portfolio. Stock options maintenance is a department that can be assigned to large businesses with strong trading positions, such as Forex.

Chapter 14: Active Income Vs Passive Income

These are the two types that can be earned. Many people are familiar with the terms passive and activate income. But many don't know the difference or how to generate passive revenue on their own.

Many people believe that knowing how passive income can be the key to wealth accumulation and financial independence. According to these people, "The key to financial independence and great wealth is the ability or skill to turn earned income into portfolio income and passive income."

What is the definition active income?

A service is a way to make money. You can earn a salary, commissions and tips by providing that service. Two other sources of active income are self-employment earnings and salary.

To generate passive income, one must have active income. Real estate investors are often able to work full-time in order to generate active income. Then, they reinvest the money to create a passive stream of income through rental properties.

Let's look at some passive income examples.

Hourly earnings are one of the most common ways to generate income from part-time and full-time jobs. One of the many benefits of being paid hourly is the possibility of earning more revenue through overtime, weekends, holidays, etc.

Salary is a predetermined amount paid to an employee in return for their regular work schedule. It could be 8-5 from Monday through Friday. The salary-paying employees give up 40 hours of work in exchange for a guaranteed source of income.

Another source of income is commissions. However, the amount of money earned can vary depending upon the type of work performed. One example is that of a realty agent. They are often paid a commission between 3 and 6 percent of the selling price of a property. A lease commission equals one month's rent. People who are only paid commissions, on the contrary, often see their revenue streams fluctuate according to the time and number of transactions.

Tips are a form passive income that is earned based on the quality of services provided. Food service and hospitality workers are often paid an hourly or a set salary. They also receive tips from satisfied customers.

There are two other sources of passive income: fees for freelance work and consultancy. To supplement their income, people with high-demand skill sets, such software engineers or graphic designers can start freelancing businesses and work as contractors for clients.

What is passive Income and how does this work?

Passive income comes from an income-producing property that is not being actively managed, such a rental property. This asset is usually acquired using savings from earnings, salaries or other forms.

Not only will you save time, but also money. Investors won't pay Medicare or Social Security taxes on passive income. Investors can take advantage of tax deductions to reduce their income tax liability.

Here are some passive income examples to get you going:

The most common ways to earn interest income are to place money in a certificate, or hold a bond, or any other financial instrument. The issue with many assets is that their interest rates are lower than the inflation. An investor could lose his principal by investing in passive income-generating assets.

Other passive income sources include dividends received from publicly listed companies. Apple, Mastercard, Nike and Nike are just a few of the prominent blue-chip businesses that pay out dividends. It can be more profitable to invest as a silent partner in business or real-estate ventures to generate passive income. Additionally, the potential returns from recurring revenue are more substantial and a part of the profits is distributed among the partners if the firm is sold.

Chapter 15: Habits Of Investing: Getting Used To It

Increasing your investment

There are always opportunities for investment growth. You should always seek out bigger opportunities, whether you've received additional income or a chance to own an asset that could be used for investment. As an investor, you should see your extra asset not as a burden but a means to increase your returns. As an example, 10% could be used to invest, but you might increase that number to 15% and 20% later.

Your mindset is both your ally and foe. It is important to have a positive mindset to encourage you to invest more. You can make your investment more profitable with these simple strategies.

1. Seek out the lowest fees. We mentioned in the previous chapter that passive investing is a good strategy. When you start to get comfortable with the process of investing, you'll soon realize that it is possible to continue using the strategy forever if you can afford it. You can become blinded to the fees you pay on investment transactions. It is important to seek out the lowest fees. To build your reputation in financial services, you must aim to have the lowest fees. There are many online brokerages that have low or no annual fees, depending on the investment requirement.

2. We've already discussed in Chapter 2 the importance of saving money on unnecessary expenses, even if it only costs a few hundred dollars. This principle also applies to investment. Even if it is only 1% or less, it can make a significant difference in the performance of portfolios. Although

it might not be immediately apparent, consider the annual fees per investment transaction you are paying.

For example, if your investment earns an average 15% per year but you pay 3% investment fees in all forms, you will only see a 12% return. While this may seem like a huge return, it is actually a very small amount when you consider the value of the money that you have invested. It is possible to make thousands of dollars more if you lower the amount of fees you pay. It is important to remember that investment expenses should be considered.

3. Market continuity – Regular contributions to your investments play a major role. Even if your market isn't performing well, you need to be consistent with how you invest your assets. This is the best approach to increasing your market share. When it comes market

conditions, some investors react too fast. All investors want to increase their wealth. It is important to not allow your goals and objectives to be diverted by how the market is performing except on rare occasions.

4.

5. Long-term thinking. - We've discussed several times in this book how to view the investment as an opportunity for your money grow over time. But, you must avoid the "get rich quickly" mindset. There are no quick returns in investment. You must be patient about the outcome. Imagine those who invest in education. Although they may not see immediate results after a few years of hardwork and setbacks, they still earn their degree. Long-term goals can be achieved through both business and monetary investments. There is no businessman who thought they would open a business for a few short

years before closing it down. An investor who succeeds knows that their goal is to be a successful one will likely be achieved if they have a long term mindset.

Everyone should always look for investment opportunities. Your investment should not be measured in terms of months or years. Instead, look for opportunities that will allow you to grow your capital over the long-term.

Investing with the right team and in a more diverse portfolio

Many investors believed that investment opportunities were a "one-man" game. However, many investors aren't aware of the importance of having a team to invest. Be aware that a successful investor is able to pick and form a team to invest.

This principle applies to all investments, not just monetary. Professional architects and designers are ideal for a team that is involved in real estate investment. They will design the houses. They will also give you advice on what to do.

How to make your investment grow. You will be able to make better decisions about how you allocate your funds in the markets if you are part of a group for monetary investment.

When you work with a team, instead of working alone, you can learn from each other and share your expertise. You won't be forced to make wrong decisions. A second benefit is the ability to share information with your team members and discuss any decisions that you might make. Trustworthiness and reliability are key components of a team. Five components are essential for investment management.

1. Team Structure

In investing, diversity has been a constant theme. Diversity should not only apply to your investment, it should also be applicable to your team. A team is made up of specialists in different fields. If you have five members in your team, that's 5 people. One person excels at forecasting, and the other excels in analyzing. Each player has one vision: make your money more. Studies have shown that working in a team can reduce the chances of you missing an opportunity in investment. This will help strengthen your foundation. Keep in mind that teams must still be balanced and aligned. It is important to be in sync, with your fellow teammates. You can either join a team with other investors or create your own.

2. Decision Rights

A team could run into problems with their decision rights. The decision rights of a team may be hampered by a portfolio manager, investment officer, or someone who is responsible for directing the team to take a single action. It is important to keep in mind that the team should always be in sync. It means that everyone should agree on all decisions. Every move made by a member of the group should bring the team to victory and not just for him.

This component is one of most difficult processes investors have to go through. Investors also prefer to play the game by themselves.

In decision making, trust and clarity play an important role. Your portfolio manager should be trusted as a teammate if you have granted him a role. The recommended team size for an investment team is between four and six people, in order to avoid any competition or too much diversity.

3. Team Philosophy & Discipline

What makes your team unique from other teams. It's the way that you play the game. Each investor may have the exact same chess pieces. However, investors differ in how they move them. Because of their approach and discipline, some investors achieve success in investing. Others believe their market-leading strategies and approach are what made them successful. They are also known for their patience with investments. It doesn't matter how disciplined your team is, but it does not matter how they value those disciplines.

These philosophies or disciplines are called Buy Discipline. This refers to how the team works and uses its managerial skills in order to buy securities or other investments. Investors can choose from 3,600 US public companies. These public companies are different in their philosophies. Investors could then align their investments with these companies' philosophies. Investments should be chosen by teams that reflect their philosophy. If they believe in the food industry, for example, they might invest in food companies.

4. Selling Decisions

One team has completed choosing and buying their investment. The next step is to sell them. Selling investments is not an easy task. You should take into account many things when you sell an investment. Asking questions such as, "Is this the best time to list or why is it performing poorly?" will help you identify which asset should be sold. You can better analyze your investments by being part of a team. You should also share the profit and dividends that you earn from selling your investments. You should always remember that it is a smart move to prepare a presentation and data that will allow all team members to agree on a single decision.

5. Continuous improvement, assessment

Every member of your staff should be able adapt to changes in the market. This includes the contribution of each person to learning. It is best to examine the situation after selling an investment. You can ask questions such as "Did you all benefit from the selling?" It can be used to assist the team in improving their decision-making skills in future investments.

Apart from building the right people, we also discuss in previous chapters how important diversification is for your investments. It is important to know how you can invest in the correct approaches. An investor who succeeds in investing knows how research works and is flexible about the methods he or she uses in the financial marketplace.

Keep in mind that your investment decisions should always take into account the facts of the situation, not your emotional attachments. Focusing on the various investment options will help you create a more diverse portfolio. This will give you more information about why you should choose an asset.

Keep to your plan

The one thing that investors often fail to do is stick with their plans. Stay committed to a team if it is something you chose. If you are determined to play the game on your own, keep at it. When their plan fails, most investors give up. While most investors feel the need to escape losses in their investments, they are not able to see that successful investors recognize that each investment has its own season. They are highly emotionally tolerant to the ups or downs in the financial industry.

According to a study in 2008, the financial crisis caused stocks to plummet by nearly half. Those who stayed put received more rewards. Those who stayed saw a 147% increase in their financial wealth. Because they purchased stocks during its decline and waited for its recovery a decade later, this is why the financial growth was so high. A study found that 25% to 25% of investors who sold stock after the financial crisis failed to return to the stock markets. It means they lost their way and didn't stick with their plans.

You can trust your own judgement and those around, and your plan will be successful. If you have doubts regarding the investment plan you've created, you can get the assistance of a professional in the financial or business world. These are the reasons financial advisors are on the market. They will help you select the best plan for your needs.

Your plan should have a single goal. But this doesn't necessarily mean that you have to set a single goal for every failure. But, sticking to your plan does not mean you cannot be flexible in your strategies. It is important to stick to your plan and not adjust based on market performance or emotions. Your strategies are carefully planned. Your circumstances may force you to abandon your hard-earned work. If you have to make difficult decisions, keep your head up and be objective. Remember, a successful investor knows when to wait and when to stick to his plans.

Choose the person that you should trust

People are visual beings. They become more visual-oriented when they see something. Be careful who you listen. It is important to seek advice from real professionals in the field, not someone who claims to be. An investor who is successful will research before investing. Financial fraudsters and investment scammers exist everywhere. They can manipulate you to take your assets. They can take many forms of investment frauds. They may be spread via email or social media, word-of mouth, phone calls, and even email. You need to be cautious about who and what you trust. According to an Australian study, there were 24% more scams reported in 2018 than 2018. This is alarming because it shows that people are being conned by these scammers.

You might have heard it from some friends. Another thing to remember is that there is no instant return. These scams are also common among our friends. Four common investment scams are possible to encounter during your journey to investment.

1. Advance Fee Scheme- Victims are persuaded into paying a specified amount of cash in exchange for a significant sum of money. However, the scammer robs victims of their money and takes it.

2. Boiler Room Scam. This scam is made up of a group who create a sample office known as the "boiler chamber". These scammers are trying to convince victims that they have a legitimate company. In order to get their victims to invest, they may create a fake company website. Even though they do their best to present a legitimate company, everything about it is fake. Their victims will soon realize that

the company they are trying to scam is fake and they will move elsewhere where they can do the same trick again.

3. Forex Scam – The Forex Market (Forex Market) is the largest financial marketplace in the world. Scammers seek victims in this market, which is why many scammers target it. It is illegal to trade forex. The majority of forex trading services operate online from another country. Foreigners are the most common victims. They believe that these trading services can be trusted. They would then end up paying the wrong people and falling for this scam. Scammers are often online and it can be difficult to track them down.

4. Offshore Investing Scam – This is a scam that entitles the victim to transfer their money offshore to another country and promises a huge return. Many people who fall for this scam want to avoid higher

taxes. This is fine as most investors are careful with their expenses. You may not be allowed to recover your money if you invest offshore.

5. Scamming with Pensions - This scam targets those who wish to make a retirement plan. You save money on your pension plan until you reach certain age. You can't withdraw your money at this point. You will be shown ads that allow you to bypass tax laws. The scammer would then promise to pay your loan back with a profit of 60-70%.

6. Ponzi Schemes or Pyramid Schemes - This is the most popular scam in the world. This scam works by recruiting people through social media sites, emails, and ads. Victims are promised large sums of money in a matter of weeks by inviting a friend. These victims often fall prey to this scheme because they know their loved ones. Scammers will convince you that this

scheme is real and give you the money for the first few week.

Because victims feel they are making a lot of money in a short time, they will be more likely to refer their friends and relatives to help them in the future. The problem is that there is no investment and the cheques victims receive are made from money given by other victims. The scammers won't give you any more cheques, and they will simply disappear taking all the money they have from their victims. This scheme is the most popular for scamming because the scammers can make a quick buck and feel real until they realize they are in danger.